Guide to Managing

Grant Funded Projects

Guide to Managing
Grant Funded Projects

Jenny Middleton
Stuart Billingham
Kath Bridger

Middlesex
University
P R E S S

First published in 2006 by Middlesex University Press

Copyright © Jenny Middleton, Stuart Billingham and Kath Bridger

ISBN 1 904750 48 6

A CIP catalogue record for this book is available from
The British Library

Design by Helen Taylor

Printed and bound by Ashford Colour Press

Middlesex University Press
North London Business Park
Oakleigh Road South
London N11 1QS

Tel: +44 (0)20 8411 5734: +44 (0)20 8411 4162
Fax: +44 (0)20 8411 5736

www.mupress.co.uk

Foreword

Aargh – handbooks. They are everywhere. Handbooks for tutors, for exams, for students, for quality, for training, for new staff, old staff, no staff...Most are too big for the hand, they don't read like books, and you can't hand them on... Does anyone know what's in them? Is there a handbook of handbooks somewhere?

So wrote Martin Coyle of Cardiff University in *The Times Higher Educational Supplement* of 13 January 2006.

Well, here is another handbook, without apologies.

I have been involved over many years both as a giver and as a receiver of funds. I am all too aware of the misunderstandings that can arise on both sides of that divide, and also particularly of the difficulties that some projects have in fulfilling their admirable aims. It is never an easy matter. But there are ways in which to succeed, and this handbook (begging your pardon) is intended to help those on both sides of the divide, but particularly those who have succeeded in attracting significant financial support, who want to fulfil their objectives, who want to be properly accountable to their funders, and who then find themselves either fully succeeding in every respect or, possibly, encountering problems not altogether foreseen. I hope it may be useful to funders as well, in following up all their good intentions.

We are much indebted to Middlesex University, where Jenny Middleton initiated this project, and to York St John University College, where she completed it. Both these organisations are committed to promoting capacity building and to learning from experience, and would hope to see success for all parties in funded projects in the voluntary sector, in schools, in further and in higher education. To all of these we commit this project and, as Mowgli would have said, 'Good hunting' to all concerned.

And thanks too to Martin Coyle, to whom this handbook is respectfully and cautiously dedicated.

Robin Guthrie
Chair of Governors, York St John University College

Contents

CHAPTER ONE

Planning a project to meet a need

Over the last thirty years millions of pounds have been wasted on devising, developing and managing projects that have not attracted the number of beneficiaries that were originally projected. There are a number of reasons a project might fail in this way. One reason is that the project was not marketed successfully – marketing activities may have been carried out but they failed to reach the target audience or to attract their attention. Perhaps a more fundamental reason for failure is that the project was not designed in a way that genuinely met the wider and holistic needs of the beneficiary group, and therefore was not of interest to them.

Projects that are either poorly designed or unsuccessfully marketed represent not only waste of money but a missed opportunity to improve quality of life for those most in need. Getting it right – designing and marketing a project that genuinely responds to the needs of those it seeks to help, and is attractive to them – represents a level of excellence that sadly is all too rare in grant-funded projects.

Marketing is covered in detail in Chapter 3. This chapter concentrates on what can be done at the planning stage in order to ensure that the project meets a genuine need and is set up and run in a way that will turn out to be successful.

This chapter introduces a number of techniques and strategies to help ensure that a project can be designed to meet a genuine need and take into account the opinions of those who will benefit from it. Although a number of research techniques are discussed, this is not an authoritative text on research methods and can do no more than skim the surface. If substantial or complex research is needed as part of a project, it is always best to involve experienced researchers. The purpose of this chapter is to give the project manager enough information to draw together some quick and simple research as part of project design, or to discuss their needs more fully with a researcher.

In order to show how this will work in practice, this chapter will use a case study example. This example project may be very different from the type of project you are involved in, but the principles are the same for all projects.

> ## Case Study – Healthy Eating in Schools
>
> The Healthy Eating in Schools project aimed to target three primary schools and one secondary school in the Greatwood neighbourhood of Newtown, a town experiencing industrial decline and social deprivation. The project team would encourage pupils to eat five portions of fruit and vegetables a day through a combination of food education and activities, banning junk food snacks and replacing them with fruit, and teaching basic cookery skills to parents.

Forming and testing a hypothesis

There is no mystery to research, it is simply a question of finding out what you need to know. It may seem like an obvious thing to say, but the core of good research is being clear about what you need to find out. This can be stated as a question, for example:

'How healthy are children's diets in Greatwood?'

Or alternatively it can be phrased as a statement that you need to test to see whether or not it is true, for example:

'Children in Greatwood have unhealthy diets'

A statement like this is called a **hypothesis**.

Many projects are automatically based on a hypothesis, whether or not that hypothesis is ever tested by research, or even written down. They are just assumed to be true. For example in our case study the project team made the following assumptions.

1. 'School pupils in Greatwood do not eat enough fruit and vegetables'
2. 'Eating five portions of fruit and vegetables provides health benefits'
3. 'School pupils prefer junk food over fruit and vegetables'
4. 'Eating more fruit and vegetables will improve pupils' behaviour'
5. 'Eating more fruit and vegetables will improve pupils' educational attainment'
6. 'Schools in this neighbourhood would welcome a healthy eating project'
7. 'Parents lack basic cookery skills'

These statements may well be true, but unless they are tested or verified in some way there is always the risk that they are untrue, or that they only tell part of the story. Often the project team doesn't even realise that they have made these assumptions, they have just taken them as self-evident. So the first question a project manager or team needs to ask themselves when they come up with an idea for a project is:

What assumptions am I making in the design of this project?

Making assumptions is not necessarily a bad thing, as many of them are based on background knowledge or experience. If you are able to list the assumptions that you are making in designing the project then you will be able to sort through them and judge which ones are certainly known to be true and which ones may need to be tested with further research.

Case Study Example – Identifying and Commenting on Assumptions

In our case study example, once the team had identified the assumptions they were making they were able to devise the following table:

Assumption	Comments
1. 'School pupils in Greatwood do not eat enough fruit and vegetables'	We think this is true because of what some doctors have told us
2. 'Eating five portions of fruit and vegetables provides health benefits'	This is recommended by the UK Government
3. 'School pupils prefer junk food over fruit and vegetables'	We think this is true from observing school pupils' behaviour
4. 'Eating more fruit and vegetables will improve pupils' behaviour'	We think this is true, but don't have any proof
5. 'Eating more fruit and vegetables will improve pupils' educational attainment'	We think this is true, but don't have any proof
6. 'Schools in this neighbourhood would welcome a healthy eating project'	One school has asked for project like this. We don't know if other schools are interested yet
7. 'Parents lack basic cookery skills'	This is a guess

In the example above, the project team thought they could probably find some proof of assumptions 4 and 5 from studies that had already been carried out in other areas, or possibly in other countries. They would be using someone else's research to back up their project. This is known as **secondary research** – finding other research that is relevant to your own project and using it as supporting evidence. Assumption 2 is also backed up by secondary research. In this case, the team already knew where to find this evidence.

For assumption 1, the team would have to carry out some research of their own in order to test whether or not the assumption was correct. The team felt it was worth investing time in carrying out this research because if this assumption were wrong then there would be no point in doing the project at all. They would have to carry out this research directly on the school pupils concerned, as no one else had researched this topic within Greatwood before. This is known as **primary research**.

Assumption 1, as it stands, cannot be tested as a hypothesis. This is because it is not phrased precisely enough.

> *'School pupils in Greatwood do not eat enough fruit and vegetables'*

In this statement, we have no idea what constitutes 'enough' fruit and vegetables, and so are unable to test whether or not the statement is true. Using the government guidelines of five portions of fruit and vegetables per day, we could amend the statement to say:

> *'School pupils in Greatwood do not eat five portions of fruit and vegetables per day'*

Although this hypothesis is now clearer, it is still not clear enough. For example, if it was found that school pupils ate ten portions of fruit and vegetables every day for six days and then four portions on the seventh day, the hypothesis would be proved true even though the pupils were clearly eating enough fruit and vegetables. The project team needs to be clearer still about what constitutes enough fruit and vegetables. They could instead state:

> *'School pupils in Greatwood do not eat five portions of fruit and vegetables per day on average over the course of a typical week.'*

This is now much closer to being a hypothesis that can be tested. One last change needs to be made. The hypothesis talks about 'school pupils' but is not precise about whether this means that no pupils at all eat the required amount of fruit and vegetables, or whether the statement applies to most pupils but not all. This could be made more precise by stating what percentage of school pupils the project team think are not eating their greens:

> *'Under 25% of school pupils in Greatwood eat five portions of fruit and vegetables per day on average over the course of a typical week.'*

This is now a statement that can be tested by research. It is also a statement that, if true, justifies the whole project.

In our case study, the project team realised that if they were going to run the project as originally planned, assumption 7 (parents lack basic cookery skills) also had to be tested as a hypothesis. However, they did not feel they were able to carry out this research at the planning stage, because they were still trying to bid for funding for the project and were low on resources. Therefore, they decided to make this research a part of the project itself, and to work with parents and their children to find out their wider opinions on food and diet and how it relates to health, behaviour and educational attainment.

Secondary research sources

For the purposes of project development, secondary research can be divided into two categories:

- Research that proves the hypothesis
- Research that supports the hypothesis

Finding research that completely proves your hypothesis may be possible in some circumstances. For the hypothesis already to be proved, someone must already have formulated the same hypothesis and must have conducted recent research that showed the hypothesis to be true. In our case study, researchers would have had to have conducted research on school pupils in Greatwood within the last few years in order for the project team to be able to say that the hypothesis was already proven.

Much more likely in the world of project development is finding research that supports the hypothesis without actually proving it. For example research may have been carried out in other parts of the country, or on topics that are similar but not identical.

Case Study Example – Secondary Supporting Research

The project team wanted to assert assumption 4 in their funding bid:

'eating more fruit and vegetables will improve pupils' behaviour'

They did not think it was necessary to prove this hypothesis conclusively, but wanted to provide some kind of supporting evidence as part of the bid. They were able to find a document summarising some research that had been carried out on prisoners in the 1980s showing that their behaviour improved significantly when more fruit vegetables were included in their diet. Although this research did not prove the hypothesis above, it was enough to suggest that the results may be similar with school pupils.

Other forms of secondary research are also used in formulating project bids. For example policy papers are often quoted, especially where these contain statistics that support one or more of the assumptions that the project developers have made. Standard sources for general policy and research papers include Learning and Skills Councils (LSCs), Regional Development Agencies (RDAs), Local Authorities and Local Education Authorities. More specific supporting evidence can be found from organisations that have a more targeted focus, such as charitable organisations (Mind, Age Concern and so on) or research based organisations (Joseph Rowntree Foundation, universities).

Primary research techniques

Having formulated a hypothesis that is capable of being tested, you will need to select an appropriate method to carry out your research. In selecting which method to use you may need to consider:

- Level of accuracy needed
- Funds available to carry out the research
- The effects of carrying out the research
- The type of hypothesis you are trying to prove.

Unless your project is particularly large or high profile you are unlikely to carry out your research to the level of accuracy expected among academic or business research communities. You're more likely to want to demonstrate that your hypothesis is reasonable rather than proving it beyond all doubt. However it is worth aiming for the most rigorous methods that you can afford in terms of time and money. This is just a question of quality, as good quality research is likely to lead to a good quality project.

Not to be forgotten is the effect of carrying out the research on the client group. Some groups of people are more sensitive to being questioned than others. For example, small businesses are often targeted by public sector projects and in certain areas where there are high levels of funding, small-business owners are suspicious of what they perceive as drains on their time. In this situation, research methods that would involve extensive surveying might end up provoking hostility from small-business owners which would have a negative effect on the subsequent project. Conversely, some forms of research may have a positive effect on the target group by engaging their interest in the subject.

One of the most significant factors in selecting appropriate research techniques is the nature of the hypothesis that you are working with. For example, compare:

> 'Under 25% of school pupils in Greatwood eat five portions of fruit and vegetables per day on average over the course of a typical week.'

with

> 'School pupils are generally hostile towards fruit and vegetables.'

The first hypothesis involves counting pupils and the number of portions of fruit and vegetables they eat. A hypothesis like this would require quantitative research. The second hypothesis on the other hand involves things that cannot be so easily counted – attitudes towards fruit and vegetables. This requires qualitative research to collect information about these attitudes.

Quantitative research

Quantitative research methods were originally developed for the natural sciences to investigate natural phenomena. Quantitative research often uses observation and measurement techniques, but can also include survey methods. Qualitative research methods, on the other hand, were developed within the social sciences and include questionnaires, interviews and surveys, focus groups and case study research.

Case Study Example – Quantitative Research

The project team wanted to test the hypothesis:

'Under 25% of school pupils in Greatwood eat five portions of fruit and vegetables per day on average over the course of a typical week.'

In order to do this, they worked with a class of Year 5 pupils (9 to 10-year-olds) in Oldfield Primary School in Greatwood. With the help and support of the class teacher, each pupil kept a diary of what they ate for one week.

The results were then analysed to see what proportion of the pupils appeared to be eating five portions of fruit and vegetables a day during the week.

According to the food diaries, only seven of the thirty pupils ate five portions of fruit and vegetables per day on average during the research period – approximately 23%.

In the example above, the project team tested the hypothesis using a sample of only thirty pupils from a total of 1,200 primary and secondary school pupils attending schools in Greatwood. Among the sample group the team did manage to prove their hypothesis because only 23% of pupils were eating five portions of fruit and vegetables that week. But does this necessarily prove the hypothesis for all 1,200 pupils?

It is reasonable when carrying out research to take a sample of a large group and to conduct the research on the sample rather than on the whole group. It would be extremely expensive and time consuming to ask all 1,200 pupils in the area to keep food diaries, so a smaller group is selected and it is assumed that the behaviour of the small group will be similar to the behaviour of the group as a whole. In other words, in our example the team assumes that because this particular class are not eating their fruit and veg then it is reasonable to assume that the same is true for all the school pupils in Greatwood.

One criticism that could be levelled at this approach is that the project team selected only pupils between the ages of 9 and 10 for their sample. Perhaps pupils who are much younger or much older behave quite differently. The results of the research would have been more convincing if the team had taken a selection of pupils of all ages from 5 to 16. However a main consideration for the team was the very limited time and money available to carry out the research. To carry out this research on sample of thirty pupils covering the whole age range would clearly have been more difficult and expensive. The team had therefore compromised by choosing pupils roughly in the middle of the age range and assuming that the results would be reasonably similar for other ages.

Another assumption that the team had made was that the week covered by the research genuinely was a typical week, and that the behaviour observed in that week was similar to the behaviour shown by the research sample at other times. The team could have carried out the research over two weeks and taken an average, which would have made the research findings more convincing. Again, finance and time were taken into consideration when the decision was made to limit the research to a single week.

Although the research carried out by the project team did not produce a result that scientists would recognise as being conclusive, it was enough to demonstrate that the hypothesis was likely to be true, more or less. This was good enough for the project team as their purpose was not to produce rigorous scientific evidence but to demonstrate that their project was needed. Their research had definitely highlighted that there was a genuine problem that needed to be addressed.

Qualitative research

Qualitative research tends to result in a broader range of information and can include data about attitudes and feelings as well as factual information. Techniques that may be used include questionnaires, interviews and focus groups. One of the potential dangers of qualitative research is that the information gathered can be difficult to use because it can sometimes be unstructured and wide-ranging. As with all kinds of research it is important to be clear at the outset why the research is being carried out and what the results will be used for.

Case Study Example – Using a Questionnaire

The project team thought that there was hostility towards fruit and vegetables among school pupils in Greatwood, but that this could be changed by the project activities. As part of the project they issued a questionnaire to all the pupils taking part, aimed at finding out what their feelings were towards fruit and vegetables. They planned to ask the pupils to fill in the same questionnaire a year later after the project had finished so that they could compare the results. They would use this comparison as part of the evaluation of the project.

Questionnaire design

Designing a questionnaire is not as simple as asking a few questions. The way questions are phrased and even the way the questionnaire is set out on the page can make a significant difference to the quality of the result.

First of all, you need to be very clear about the scope of the information that the questionnaire will gather. One of the advantages of questionnaires is that they can ask a number of different questions and therefore they have the potential to collect a lot of information in a short space of time. However, there does need to be some kind of logical thinking behind the range of questions that is asked. A questionnaire that jumps from one subject to another may be confusing for the person filling it in, and a long questionnaire is likely to be boring to fill in.

Case Study Example – Designing a Questionnaire

The team agreed to design a questionnaire that would be filled in by Year 9 pupils (13 to 14-year-olds) taking part in the project. The questionnaire would include factual questions about how often the pupils ate fruit and vegetables and questions about their attitudes and feelings towards eating fruit and vegetables. The team also decided to include questions about other food types as a comparison.

There are different types of questions that may be asked on a questionnaire. One of the more important distinctions is between:

■ Open questions

■ Closed questions.

Closed questions present a limited number of choices in the way they can be answered and are therefore very useful in questionnaires. The choice may be limited to 'yes' or 'no', for example:

Do you like fruit? *Yes/No*

Alternatively, there may be a number of different options presented. For example:

Which of these fruits do you like? *Banana/Apple/Pear/Peach*

Another type of response known as the Likert Scale is often used on questionnaires, in which a statement or question is presented and the respondent has to indicate their reply from a set of choices. For example:

I like to eat fruit.

Strongly agree/Agree/Neither agree nor disagree/Disagree/Strongly disagree

OR

How confident do you feel about cooking with exotic vegetables?

Not at all confident/Somewhat unconfident/Neither confident nor unconfident/Somewhat confident/Very confident

Questions using the Likert Scale give the respondent a wide range of responses to the question but the results are still easy to classify and compare. Providing the responses are set out in order from one extreme to the other, as in the examples above, the answers can be numbered from 1-5 and an average can be calculated across all the questionnaires.

In the example above, if the average score for the question 'I like to eat fruit' is 3.45 then this easily demonstrates that the group who answered the questionnaire are slightly hostile towards fruit. A score of less than three would show a positive feeling towards eating fruit.

Open questions allow the respondent to answer the question in any way they choose. For example:

What do you think of fruit?

Questions that prompt a free-form response such as the one above can be useful in questionnaires if used sparingly and if thought is given to how the responses to these open ended questions will be used. What often happens is that open questions are included in a questionnaire and then are ignored when it comes to processing the results because the information is difficult to classify and analyse.

Both open and closed questions can be used in a questionnaire, but there are some types of questions that are best avoided:

Case Study Example – Potential Pitfalls

The project team completed a first draft of the questions to be asked on the questionnaire as follows:

1. How often do you eat fruit and vegetables?

   Never/Sometimes/Often/Very often

2. What are your favourite foods?

---

3. Do you like fruit? *Yes/No*

4. Do you like vegetables? *Yes/No*

5. Do you like crisps? *Yes/No*

6. Do you like chocolate? *Yes/No*

7. Do you like fizzy drinks? *Yes/No*

8. Do you think your diet is:

   Very healthy/Healthy/OK/Not healthy

9. What are your views on healthy eating?

---

10. How much do you weigh and how tall are you?

---

11. How many portions of fruit and vegetables did you eat last week?

This first draft was reviewed by the team and piloted with a small group of Year 9 pupils.

Following the review and pilot in the example above, the team decided to revise the questionnaire considerably.

Question 1 was just too vague and open to interpretation – one person's 'often' may be another person's 'sometimes'. The question was changed to:

1. On average how many portions of fruit and vegetables do you eat per day?

None/One or two/Between three and five/Six or more

This is far more precise and the results are more likely to be meaningful. Most of the pupils who piloted the questionnaire were not sure how much fruit or vegetables made up a 'portion', so the following wording was added to the question:

'A portion can be: one medium sized piece of fruit; or three heaped tablespoons of vegetables; or a small glass of fruit juice.'

Questions 3 – 7 were thought to be too restrictive with just yes/no answers. It was decided to phrases these questions so that they could be answered using the Likert Scale. **Question 8** would also be changed to standardise all the questions in this section. The result was as follows:

For the following questions, please circle the response that most closely matches how much you agree or disagree with the statement:

3. I like fruit	Strongly agree	Agree	Neither agree nor disagree	Disagree	Strongly disagree
4. I like vegetables	Strongly agree	Agree	Neither agree nor disagree	Disagree	Strongly disagree
5. I like crisps	Strongly agree	Agree	Neither agree nor disagree	Disagree	Strongly disagree
6. I like chocolate	Strongly agree	Agree	Neither agree nor disagree	Disagree	Strongly disagree
7. I like fizzy drinks	Strongly agree	Agree	Neither agree nor disagree	Disagree	Strongly disagree
8. I think my diet is healthy	Strongly agree	Agree	Neither agree nor disagree	Disagree	Strongly disagree

When the questionnaire was piloted, the team found that **Question 9** resulted in so many diverse answers that it was difficult to know what to do with the information except to list it. Question 9 was therefore scrapped.

The team also found that not all pupils answered **Questions 10 and 11**. One of the researchers interviewed some of the pupils to try and find out why. She found that some of the pupils had not answered the question about height and weight because they weren't sure of their height or weight. Others had not answered because they were embarrassed. In the case of Question 11, few of the pupils could remember what they had eaten last week.

Other potential pitfalls include:

- **Leading questions** that assume the answer, such as 'of course you do like crisps, don't you!' if you already know the answer you don't need to ask the question. Although the example is a very blatant one, it is possible to lead in more subtle ways by using very positive or very negative language, or by giving examples that suggest the question should be answered in a particular way. The question: 'Do you eat plenty of healthy fruit and vegetables?' is phrased in a leading way because the question hints quite strongly that the respondent should be eating fruit and vegetables.

- **Hypothetical questions** about things that might happen, like: 'Will you eat an apple tomorrow?' The answers to these questions are likely to be unreliable because what people think they will do and what they actually do can be very different. It is much more useful to ask about what people have actually done.

- **Long, complex or difficult to answer questions.** Take, for example, the following question: 'Compare the number of fruit and vegetables you ate yesterday with the number of junk food items, including fizzy drinks, that you ate. Did you eat more fruit and vegetable items than junk food items?' Not only is the question needlessly complicated but it is very long. There is a risk that respondents will not answer the question accurately because they don't understand it or because they perceive it as being too difficult or too much of a bother.

Instructions and support

As well as the questions, questionnaires need to include clear and concise instructions to help respondents answer correctly. These could include example answers as well as guidance. Some groups of respondents may need to have the instructions and in some cases the questions adapted to their needs. For example, young children, people with learning difficulties and people whose first language is not English may need questions to be phrased more simply.

Case Study Example – Adapting a Questionnaire

As well as surveying Year 9 pupils, the team wanted to adapt the same questionnaire for Year 4 pupils (8 to 9-year-olds). They decided to use the revised versions of questions 1 – 8 as they were, but instead of using the words 'strongly agree' etc, they used pictures of smiling and frowning faces instead. The two schools being surveyed had agreed that the class teacher would take the pupils through the questionnaire in lesson time. Instead of answering question 2 individually, the teacher would lead a class discussion about favourite foods and record the answers given by members of the class. Class members would also measure their height and weight as part of a science project and these would be passed on to the researchers.

Analysing the results

The project team collated all the questionnaire results – 118 in total. Taking 'strongly disagree' as 1 and 'strongly agree' as 5, the average scores for questions 3 and 4 were:

I like fruit: 3.95

I like vegetables: 2.01

In the case study example, although the pupils were negative about vegetables, as might have been expected, they were quite positive towards fruit. This gave the team something to build on and one of the results of the research was that some of the schools introduced 'fruit-only tuck shops' which proved popular as well as healthy.

Quantifying the results is important, but equally important is to ask:

- What does this result mean?
- How does it complement other information?
- What will we do differently as a result?

These questions will allow you to use the results of the research in your project design.

Focus groups

Focus groups can be a useful way not only of gathering information, but also of ensuring that the people your project seeks to help feel that they have been consulted rather than having a project imposed on them. Running a true focus group is a skill that can only be developed over time and is perhaps best left to the researchers, but anyone can use and adapt focus group techniques to carry out a consultation and to gain useful insights into the needs of the potential beneficiaries.

Setting up and running a focus group generally involves the following stages, which can also be adapted for one-to-one interviews:

- **Preparation.** Focus groups are usually run with between six and twelve participants. These need to be selected to represent the beneficiary group as a whole. Thought should be given to the best time of day to hold the group, and the needs of those who will participate (for example, refreshments, childcare facilities, accessible location)

- **Schedule.** Groups are usually run as semi-structured interviews. This means that although the researcher will have a list of topics to be covered and questions to be asked (an interview schedule), they are prepared to let the discussion range a little. All questions that are prepared should be as open as possible. Try not to introduce too many topics (probably four to six would be enough).

- **Informed consent.** Those who are to take part in the focus group should be informed as far as possible about why the research is taking place, and should agree in writing to take part. It is usual to assure participants that their identities will be kept anonymous. This means that, in order to act ethically, the researcher must ensure that individuals cannot be identified in any of the research documentation such as transcripts or research reports. When quoting participants, it is common to give them pseudonyms or identify them just by their age and gender (and ethnic group, if this is important to the research).

- **Setting up the group.** The room to be used for the group should be comfortable – light, neither too hot nor too cold, neither too big nor too small. Participants and the researcher should be able to sit round in a circle with equal-status seating. It is highly recommended that you tape record the session, as it is virtually impossible to take adequate notes while managing the discussion. This means testing out the recording equipment in advance.

■ **Running the group.** The researcher should outline again the reason for the research, and assure the group that their opinions are valuable. Once the first question has been asked, the researcher can encourage the discussion by non-verbal signals (such as nodding) and asking prompting questions (for example, 'how does that make you feel?', or 'what do you think about that?') If one or two people seem to be dominating the discussion, it can be useful to ask the group if they could go round in turn and each say something about the topic under discussion. It is important that the interviewer respects the opinions that are being put forward – that means not registering disagreement or even disgust, whatever is said.

■ **Drawing the session to a close.** Some researchers prefer to try and summarise some of the discussion points towards the end, so that the participants have a chance to clarify or add to anything that they have said. Others prefer not to do this. At the close of the group, you should thank participants for their time and contribution, and where possible promise to send them a copy of any report or other result of the research. It goes without saying that it is essential to follow up on this promise once it has been made.

■ **Transcribing the session.** Researchers in the social sciences generally make a full typed transcription of the session for analysis, and if time and resources permit, this is the best way to go about analysing the results. It may be more cost-effective for a skilled audio-typist to make the transcription.

■ **Analysing the results.** When working with a transcription, it is usual to code different sections depending on the themes that emerge during the course of the discussion. This will allow you at a later date to see how many times a particular theme or topic is discussed, and what is being said about it. If you do not have a transcription, you could work directly from the tape and identify themes and quotations of interest. However, if working this way it is doubly important to avoid bias, as it would be easy to focus on the themes that are of interest while ignoring those that do not fit with the project.

How you deal with the results depends on the purpose of the research and how the results will be used. For example, a piece of focus group research might be used to find out how a group of 'Access to Higher Education' learners feel about making the move to Higher Education at the end of their course. Themes that crop up repeatedly during the course of their discussion (for example, anxiety about being able to cope with the level of work at university) may be discussed in different ways and in different contexts, but an analysis of the transcript will allow the researcher to identify and code the different comments and discussions as belonging to the same theme. This gives an insight into what is important to the individuals involved and what is on their mind at the present time.

Case Study Example – Focus Groups

The project manager for the Healthy Eating in Schools project conducted a focus group with eight parents. The discussion was wide ranging and allowed the parents to discuss their views on food, eating and their children's diets quite widely. The following section of dialogue was taken from the transcript of the session, and involved a dialogue between Betty, a woman in her early 30s, and Julie, a woman in her mid-40s. Both had two children of primary school age.

Betty: But it's, like, you know, they come in from school and it's like, 'chips, I want chips', innit?

Julie: Yeah, but in our house it's like, 'tough, we're having this', you know?

Betty: But then you think, well maybe they won't eat nothing. You don't want them going hungry.

Julie: You want them to eat, but you want them to eat the right things too. Cos you don't know what some of that stuff is doing to them, and then you think, well maybe it's worse for them to eat, you know, like crisps and chocolate and all that, than not have anything.

Betty: But you don't want them starving

Julie: Kids won't starve themselves. Mine will eat fruit and they will eat vegetables, because they know they're not having chips every day.

Betty: And you can't force feed them sprouts and carrots all the time, they…(interrupted)

Julie: No, but you can find some healthy things they like, can't you.

> In this section of dialogue, the project manager was able to identify an important theme that cropped up throughout the focus group – parents being anxious about their children not eating. In several parts of the meeting, some of the parents had mentioned that they would rather give the children food that they liked, even if it was unhealthy, than risk them going hungry. This information gave the team an important insight into the genuine fears of parents, and prompted them to work with parents to find healthy foods that were easy to cook and that the children liked.
>
> Note that the transcription records exactly what was said. There is no attempt to correct grammar or to rephrase anything.

Using research to improve a project

As has been stressed repeatedly throughout this chapter, the results of any research should be used to plan and design the project so that it is both useful and attractive to those at whom it is aimed. Results may come out of the research that challenge your existing views about how the project should be run, or those of other team members or project partners. Without a willingness to change there is little point in engaging in research and this should be made clear to everyone at the outset. But if everyone is prepared to keep an open mind until the results are in, engaging in appropriate research can be an extremely powerful way of ensuring that the project will be a success in both the short and the long term.

Summary

Conducting research is a good way to ensure that the project meets a genuine need.

All projects are based on assumptions. If these assumptions can be identified then they can be turned into hypotheses that can be tested by research.

Secondary research is more likely to support, rather than to prove, a hypothesis. However, this may be enough for the purposes of the project.

Primary research can be used to prove a hypothesis, or to gain more information about the opinions and thoughts of potential project beneficiaries.

Research may be **quantitative** or **qualitative**. Quantitative research generates numbers and statistics, whereas qualitative research generates larger quantities of rich information that cannot be quantified.

Questionnaires can be used to collect both quantitative and qualitative data. Questionnaires should be well planned and questions phrased clearly. Both open and closed questions can be used.

Closed questions can use a yes/no answer, or a Likert scale. Open questions should be used sparingly, and thought given in advance as to how the results will be used.

Ideally, questionnaires should be piloted and refined.

Focus groups can be used to generate qualitative data that will give an insight into the thoughts and feelings of the target group. They are also a good way of ensuring that people feel they have been consulted.

Results of research can and should be used to improve the design of a project, even if this challenges the existing ideas of the project team and partners.

Further reading

Langdridge, D (2004) *Research Methods and Data Analysis in Psychology*, Pearson.

CHAPTER TWO

Project scheduling and management techniques

A project can be a daunting thing. Keeping track of all the different tasks involved in delivering the project isn't something you can just do in your head however hard you try – that's a recipe for sleepless nights!

A great deal of 'science' has grown up around the subject of project management, with complex tools and techniques designed to manage and monitor every aspect of a project. This is what most people think of when they talk about project management – formal schedules and charts that help the project manager to monitor their progress and to take action if things start to drift.

In reality, formal project planning techniques are an essential technique for managing projects but they are by no means the whole story, as the other chapters in this book demonstrate. Nonetheless, without some way of keeping on top of the project's progress there is a significant likelihood that the project will fail in some way – either it will go over budget, will not be delivered on time or it will fail to do what it set out to do.

These three factors – time, money (and other resources) and outcome – are known as constraints. They are usually set at the planning stage and there may be very little, if any, room for change once the project has started. This is especially the case with grant funded projects where it is very rare for additional money to be granted once the project has started.

The science of project management involves planning within the confines of these constraints and balancing them on a day-to-day basis. The three constraints are often depicted as a project resources triangle:

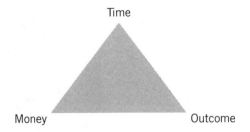

Time

Money   Outcome

The purpose of showing the constraints in this way is to demonstrate how interconnected they are. A change in the amount of time available to carry out the project will have some impact on the money required and the outcomes that can be achieved, and so on. For this reason, incidentally, it is important that if as a result of bidding for funds a change is made by the funding body – for example that less money is granted than was originally requested – then the project team should enter into serious negotiations about what can realistically be achieved and by when. If necessary, a whole new project plan should be drawn up. This will help to eliminate one of the more common reasons for project failure.

The project schedule

A **project schedule** is a graphical or tabular representation of the tasks involved in the project, plotted against time. The simplest way to capture this information is in a table or on a calendar. However, for all but the smallest projects it may be difficult to summarise all the necessary information in this way. More formalised ways of drawing up a project schedule have been developed over the years, arising initially from the engineering and construction industries. Two of the most well known are PERT charts and Gantt chart. Both can be very useful to the manager of public, voluntary or community sector projects and can be adapted to suit the needs and scope of the project.

In formal project management terms, the project schedule is part of a more comprehensive planning cycle that includes:

■ Drawing up an initial project **specification**

■ Gaining **authorisation** for the specification

■ Drawing up a **project plan** (this includes the project schedule)

■ Obtaining the appropriate **resources**

■ **Monitoring** the project on an ongoing basis

■ **Replanning** in order to adapt to change.

A project specification sets out what the project aims to achieve and how it will achieve it. This is best done before the bid or proposal is even submitted to the potential funder, as much of the necessary information will be included in the bid and will be used by the funding body to assess the project's potential and viability. Thus for social and regeneration projects, gaining authorisation for a project specification translates into submitting a bid which is then approved for funding[1].

If you are working on a project that has not been clearly specified, refer to Chapter 8: *Taking on a project part way through*, in order to gather the information needed to draw up a useful project schedule.

---

1   For a more detailed look at drawing up a project specification, see Middleton, J (2003) *Guide to Bidding*, Middlesex University Press. ISBN 1898253897

As noted on the list above, the project schedule forms a part of a wider project plan, a formal document that will include the following:

- The project's aim and objectives

- Outputs and outcomes

- The team and reporting structure of the project within the organisation or partnership, including the terms of reference for any steering or management group (see Chapter 5)

- How the project will be implemented

- Procedures that will be used

- A project schedule.

Whether or not to draw up a formal project plan is an individual decision for the project manager. It may be useful for larger projects, those that are to be closely monitored by the funding body or those that include a number of partners. For small projects, or those that have been run before, it may be more effort than it is worth.

However it is always worth drawing up some kind of project schedule. Some of the many reasons for investing time and effort into scheduling include:

- The setting of clearly defined objectives at all stages

- Management and partner involvement

- Commitment from the project team

- Tracking of the project's financial situation

- Tracking of outputs achieved

- Accurate estimates of resource needs

- A framework for monitoring that identifies and manages change.

So the schedule is not only a tracking tool for the project manager but also a management tool with wider applications.

Case Study – Skills Audits for SMEs

The Skills Audit Project aimed to carry out a skills needs analysis questionnaire on thirty small to medium sized enterprises (SMEs) to provide each one with a report on suitable training and development opportunities and to produce an overall research report to inform future policy in the region.

The project was given funding by the local Learning and Skills Council (LSC), who asked for the project to be completed within six months rather than nine months as had originally been planned. Therefore it was essential for the project team to draw up a specification, firstly to ensure that the project was still viable at all, and secondly to make sure that they delivered all the outputs and therefore could claim all the funding.

Creating a schedule

The basis of creating a project schedule is to break down the project into its individual tasks and link these together in a logical way. There are different ways of linking this information together in a diagram, and each method highlights different information about the project. However, they all start with this basic project breakdown.

One of the ways to do this is to start with a mind map. A mind map is a way of thinking through a project (or indeed any topic) that allows the mind to wander along a number of different paths at the same time, and to jot down whatever comes to mind. The mind map may include many of the tasks that need to be carried out within the project, but it may also include other information such as reminders, ideas, useful contacts and partner organisations and so on. The idea at this stage is to begin the process of thinking things through.

Case Study Example – Mind Map

The project manager created the following mind map while initially thinking about the project:

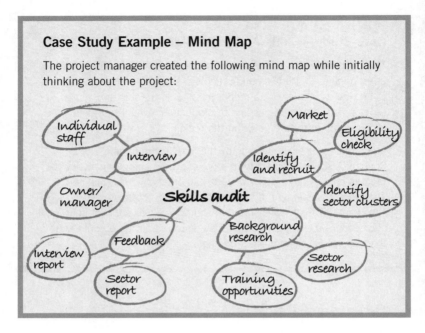

This exercise creates an overview and allows you to jot down ideas as they come to mind, grouped around themes or issues within the project. The benefit of using a mind map is that it takes the mind away from thinking in straight lines about sequences of tasks and opens it to more creative possibilities and wider considerations. For this reason it is more valuable to many people than, for example, making a list.

It is important when carrying out this mind map exercise not to become bogged down in the details of any particular task at this stage – that can come later. Neither is it important to think about who will be carrying out the tasks. Even tasks that will be carried out by a partner organisation should be included at this stage.

Mind maps can be used by the project manager alone as part of the work of scheduling, but they are perhaps more valuable still when the whole team is involved, including partner organisations that will be involved in the delivery of the project.

Work Breakdown Schedule

A **Work Breakdown Schedule** (WBS) is a more formal method than a mind map and focuses entirely on tasks. A WBS organises tasks within the project into smaller and smaller sub-tasks, represented as a tree diagram. A WBS may take some of its information from a mind map, but is likely to develop it much further.

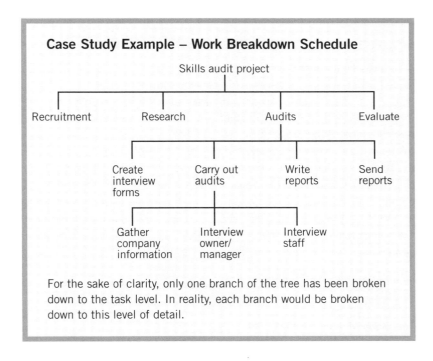

Case Study Example – Work Breakdown Schedule

Skills audit project

Recruitment   Research   Audits   Evaluate

Create interview forms   Carry out audits   Write reports   Send reports

Gather company information   Interview owner/manager   Interview staff

For the sake of clarity, only one branch of the tree has been broken down to the task level. In reality, each branch would be broken down to this level of detail.

Grouping the tasks hierarchically in this way makes it easier to assign tasks or groups of tasks to an individual or team. A task or group of tasks assigned in this way is referred to as a **work package**. Within the diagram a work package may be one of the tasks on the bottom level of the diagram or it may be one of the tasks on a higher level, which would include a number of sub tasks. A WBS enables everyone involved in the project to see where their own tasks fit in to the overall project. This can be very helpful for projects that involve a number of different staff, especially if those staff work in different departments or even different organisations. Drawing up a work package agreement (see Chapter 6) and showing how it fits in with the work of others can be an excellent motivational tool that helps keep everyone focused on the task in hand, especially if progress is regularly reviewed.

As well as being a useful tool in its own right, the WBS provides a stepping stone to creating a more comprehensive schedule. The WBS shows a full list of the tasks that need to be carried out in order to achieve the project, therefore it provides the raw material for creating a schedule that includes information about time.

Duration, dependencies and connectivity

The next step towards creating a completed schedule is to take each of the tasks in turn and add time-based information to these. This can be done with the smallest sub-tasks or with tasks at a higher level in the tree diagram, depending on how detailed you need the schedule to be. As a general guide, if the project involves work that is new to your organisation (or team) it is safest to break it down to the most detailed level – for example 'proofread report', 'produce final draft of report' and so on. If on the other hand some of the tasks are very familiar, or if they are to be carried out by others, you could work with a higher level – groups of tasks, for example 'produce and send reports'. For this reason you should read the word **task** in the following sections as representing the most appropriate level of breakdown that meets your need.

Firstly, some useful definitions:

The **duration** of a task is the length of time it takes to complete.

The **dependencies** of a task are:

- Other tasks that need to be completed before the task can start
- Other tasks that cannot start until the task is completed.

Connectivity is the linkage between different tasks based on this information.

Case Study Example – Serial String

The manager of the Skills Audit Project cannot carry out the audit until she has arranged an appointment with the SME in question, which in turn she can't do until the SME has been identified and checked for eligibility.

These tasks are dependent on one another. They represent a sequence of tasks that has to be carried out in a set order. This can be shown as a serial string like so:

identify SMEs ➡ check for eligibility ➡ set up appointments ➡ carry out audits

Other tasks could have been added to the serial string in this example. The task 'send report and list of training opportunities to SME' could have been added to the end.

You will note that it is not important to know the duration of each of these tasks in order to map the dependencies in this way. It is simply a case of saying 'this has to be finished before that can be started'.

However, projects are rarely as simple as this diagram suggests. What if some tasks from other parts of the project were also included, for example some of the research tasks. We would then have a more complex situation as not all of the tasks need to be done one after another, and yet some of the tasks may be dependent on more than one other task before they can be started.

A good way to work this out is to set up a table listing each of the tasks you want to consider, and then going through the table asking 'what other tasks must be completed before this can be started'. The table can be used to consider a small group of tasks, perhaps the breakdown of one of the main branches of the WBS, or indeed all of the tasks in the project.

Case Study Example – Dependency Table

The example below shows a group of tasks from the Skills Audit Project. The column labelled 'dependent on' is used to record the number of any tasks that the task in that row is directly dependent on. This column is sometimes labelled 'predecessors'.

Task number	Task description	Dependent on
01	Identify SMEs	
02	Check for eligibility	01
03	Set up appointments	02
04	Carry out audits	03
05	Send reports	04,08
06	Research sector background	
07	Research training opportunities	
08	Write up report	04,06,07

A table of this kind is easily scalable to encompass the largest of projects. It can be worked over several times in order to ensure that all the dependencies have been captured, because it is easy to miss some of them the first time through.

You will notice that in the example above, each task has been given its own unique identification number. This is a useful way of tracking dependencies because numbers can be used instead of lengthy task descriptions.

Another thing you may notice is that although task number 04 cannot be started before task number 01 is completed, task 01 is not listed in the 'Dependent on' column for task 04. This is because tasks 01 – 04 form a serial string, as we saw earlier. Anything dependent on task 03 is automatically also dependent on task 02, which in turn is dependent on task 01. Because they follow in this logical sequence, saying that something is dependent on task 03 is the same as saying it is dependent on task 01 then task 02 then task 03.

All of this becomes much clearer if it is drawn up into a diagram.

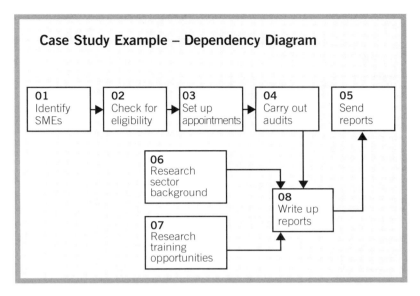

A diagram such as this is extremely useful. It allows the project manager to see at a glance which tasks have to be done first, and therefore which tasks need to be prioritised. It also shows which tasks can be done at the same time and so can perhaps be given to different people to work on in order to get the project done faster. In the example above, one staff member could be identifying SMEs and setting up appointments while someone else, perhaps even another organisation, undertakes the research tasks.

One of the most helpful aspects of a dependency diagram in practice is that it sets all this information down on paper so that the project manager and other staff don't get caught in a common procrastination trap of putting off the project because they are not sure where to start.

However, to make the diagram even more useful, information about the duration of each task can also be included. As with dependencies, it is easier to capture this information in table form first of all.

Case Study Example – Table with Duration and Dependencies

Task number	Task description	Duration (in days)	Dependent on
01	Identify SMEs	5	
02	Check for eligibility	1	01
03	Set up appointments	2	02
04	Carry out audits	20	03
05	Send reports	3	08
06	Research sector background	8	
07	Research training opportunities	8	
08	Write up report	3	04,06,07

In the above example, information about duration is given in days, but this is not compulsory. It may be more useful to some projects to give durations in weeks rather than days and this is absolutely fine as long as one measure is used consistently throughout. (How to estimate the duration of a task is a subject in its own right. Ideally it should be done at the early planning stage, and is covered elsewhere[2].)

This information about the duration of each task can be added to the dependency diagram to turn it into a PERT chart.

PERT charts

PERT stands for Programme Evaluation and Review Technique. The technique in its entirety can be very complex and statistical, but when most people talk about PERT they are referring to PERT charts, a useful way of recording project schedule information. Also known as a **network diagram**, a PERT chart maps out the dependencies between project tasks, and takes account of durations in order to be able to predict start and end dates for all the tasks in a project.

The Dependency Diagram shown above was a simplified version of a PERT chart. It can easily be adapted to include information about the duration

2 Middleton, J (2003) *Guide to Bidding*, Middlesex University Press. ISBN 1898253897

as well as the dependencies of each task. More importantly, it can then be plotted against real time, so that each task has a start and end date which links in with start and end dates of other tasks.

Instead of a simple box with the task number and name, a PERT chart contains information about the duration of each task and the start and end date of the task. There are variations on how this information is presented, but a common and useful way of doing so is given below.

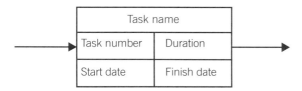

Working out the start and end dates is no trivial exercise as it depends in part on how many people are involved in carrying out the project, because if several people (or organisations) are involved then there is the potential for some tasks to be carried out simultaneously. In project management speak, resources (in other words, people) now need to be included. Again, a table will be useful in order to capture this information.

Case Study Example – Table with Dependencies, Duration and Resources

Task number	Task description	Duration (in days)	Dependent on	Resource
01	Identify SMEs	5		Kim
02	Check for eligibility	1	01	Kim
03	Set up appointments	2	02	Kim
04	Carry out audits	20	03	Kim
05	Send reports	3	08	Sacha
06	Research sector background	8		Carmel
07	Research training opportunities	8		Carmel
08	Write up report	3	04,06,07	Carmel

The resource information in the table overleaf is important because, together with the dependency information, it allows the project manager to work out which tasks can be carried out at the same time.

To illustrate how all this information can be captured, the diagram below shows the case study example project as a PERT chart.

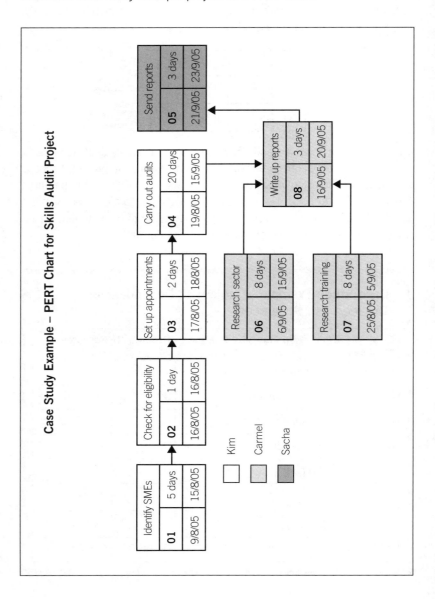

Case Study Example – PERT Chart for Skills Audit Project

In the example, the tasks have been colour coded to make it clearer who will be carrying them out. This is not strictly necessary but may be helpful.

Critical path

Because two of the groups of tasks: 01 – 04 and 06 – 07 are not dependent on each other **and** they are being carried out by different people then they can take place at the same time. In this way, a list of tasks that adds up to fifty days in total can be done in less time – thirty-four working days in the above example.

Task 08 cannot be done until tasks 01 – 04 and tasks 06 and 07 have been done. Tasks 01 – 04 will take twenty-eight days whereas tasks 06 and 07 only take sixteen days. Therefore from the project's start date, Carmel has twelve days **slack**. She could either start her tasks twelve days after the project's start date, as in the example, or start them at the beginning of the project and take a twelve-day break before starting task 08. Of course it would probably be advisable for her to start the tasks early just in case something crops up that causes her to be delayed.

The longest continuous chain of tasks that are dependent on one another is: 01-02-03-04-08-05, adding up to thirty-four days. There is no slack in this chain and so as things stand the project cannot be done in any less than thirty-four working days. In project management terms, this is known as the **critical path**.

Even though three people are involved in tasks on the critical path, this will not make the chain shorter than if the same person was doing all the tasks. Sacha, for example, is entirely dependent on Kim and Carmel finishing their tasks before he can carry out his one task. If either of them is delayed, task 05 is delayed and the whole project will be finished late. Therefore tasks on the critical path need to be monitored more closely by the project manager than other tasks that are not on the critical path. This can be very useful in deciding where to focus the most effort.

The only way for the critical path to be made shorter would be for an additional person to work on the tasks as well. For example, someone else could be brought in to carry out skills audits as well as Carmel. Between them they could do all the audits in half the time, cutting ten days from the critical path. This is sometimes referred to as crashing and can be useful if the project is under severe time pressure.

Creating a real-time schedule

The PERT chart in the example includes actual dates. These have been worked out to take weekends into account, with the result that the project as a whole covers a period of nearly two months. The dates have been worked out backwards from the end, along the critical path. Tasks that are not on the critical path (tasks 06 and 07) have been fitted in afterwards.

The dates given have also taken into account who will be working on the project so tasks 06 and 07 are not scheduled to take place at the same time because they will be done by the same person. However, it does not really matter in which order they are done. In fact the project manager could just as easily combine them into a single work package taking sixteen days and leave Carmel to plan the work herself within the given time period.

One thing that has not been taken into account is the other commitments of staff working on the project. The example shows an ideal situation in which all staff are available 100% of the time, and take no sick leave or holiday – something that never happens in real life! The dates could be adjusted to take this into account. If someone is expected to be able to give 50% of their time to the project tasks then an eight-day task will take sixteen days. For someone working only one day a week on the project, an eight-day task would take eight weeks. And so on.

Tasks can also be scheduled to take account of times when people are not going to be available. Sometimes this might influence who the tasks are given to, or perhaps it means that the whole project will take longer in order to accommodate someone whose skills are critical to the project. For tasks that are not on the critical path this is clearly less of an issue.

Another factor that has not been taken into account is delays relating to external factors. For our case study example, it would be very unusual if the small businesses involved in the project were able to meet with the project team within a day or so of being contacted. It would be more reasonable to expect at least a couple of weeks between setting up the appointments and carrying out the audits. This kind of delay is known as lag. It can be taken into account within the schedule by leaving a two week gap between tasks 03 and 04, or by including a dummy task.

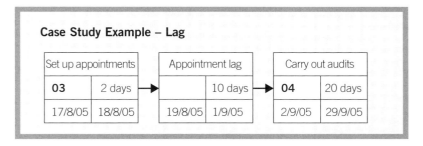

Case Study Example – Lag

Set up appointments		Appointment lag		Carry out audits	
03	2 days		10 days	**04**	20 days
17/8/05	18/8/05	19/8/05	1/9/05	2/9/05	29/9/05

Because tasks 03 and 04 are on the critical path, this lag affects the end date of the project. Lag can be built in for all kinds of known delay, for example delivery time or the time it takes for an advert to appear in the paper. Lag can also be built into the schedule to give some contingency time in case of unforeseen delays such as staff sickness.

Gantt charts

The Gantt chart uses the same basic information as a PERT chart but displays it in a different way. Instead of using boxes of information it shows tasks taking up blocks of time along a calendar, making it very easy to see what needs to be done when. Gantt charts and PERT charts tend to highlight different issues in relation to the project, and therefore it is largely a matter of personal preference which one to use. Sometimes it is useful to create one of each. *Please see charts overleaf.*

Gantt charts make it easier to include project **milestones**. A milestone is an event or achievement that is reached during the project, but unlike a task it does not take up any significant time on the schedule. Examples of milestones include:

- First steering group meeting
- Report published
- Ten students completed their training
- Thirty young people signed up for the project
- Computers installed.

Milestones are a good way to measure progress and provide clear proof that the project is on track – or not! They can also be used to motivate the whole team because they are a measure of what has been achieved to date.

A milestone is usually shown on a Gantt chart as small diamond shape. In the second chart overleaf, the Gantt chart includes a single milestone – '15 audits completed'.

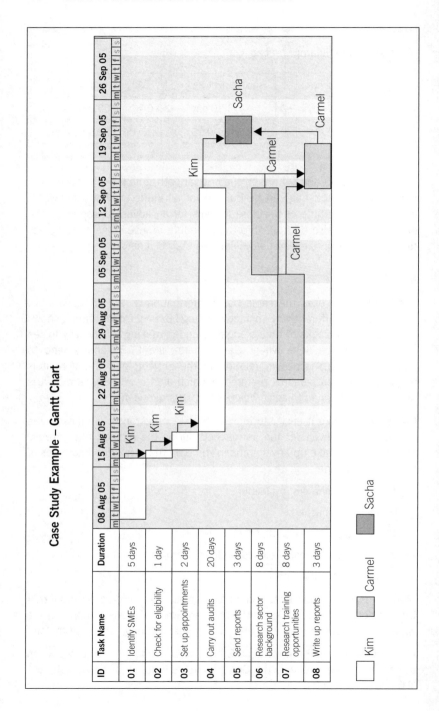

Case Study Example – Gantt Chart

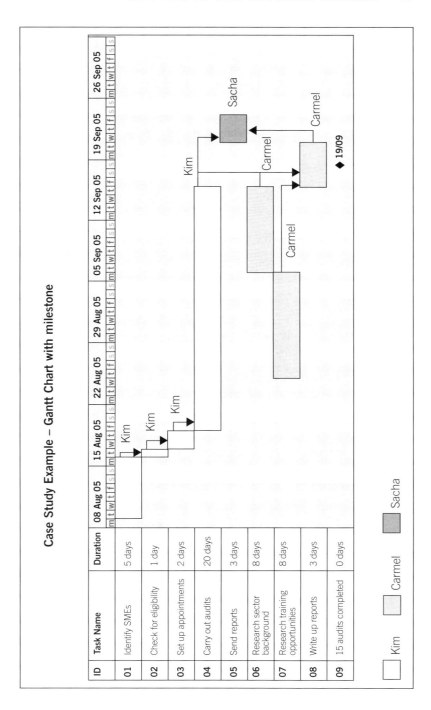

Case Study Example – Gantt Chart with milestone

Many people now use computer software to draw out Gantt and PERT charts. This can be an excellent time saver as the computer makes all the calculations about time and dates and draws out the charts for you. It is worth bearing in mind though that the resulting charts will only be as good as the information that is supplied. The work of breaking the project into tasks, estimating durations, working out dependencies and assigning resources still needs to be done, preferably before the computer is switched on.

Summary

Formal project planning techniques are an essential tool for all but the simplest of projects.

All projects are subject to the **constraints** of time, money and outcome.

A **project schedule** is a graphical representation of the tasks involved in a project plotted against time and may also include information about resources. It is useful not only for planning and monitoring a project but also as a wider management tool.

A project schedule forms part of a **project plan** which in turn is an element in the project planning cycle.

The first step towards creating a schedule is to break down the project into individual tasks. Using a **mind map** can be useful at the initial thinking stage. A more formal method is to create a **work breakdown schedule (WBS)**.

Information from the WBS can be used to map out the **dependencies** of different tasks to show how they are interconnected. Once information about the **duration** of each task has been added, this allows the whole project to be plotted against real time.

The two main methods of drawing up a schedule are **PERT charts** and **Gantt charts**. Both require the same basic information. PERT charts show very clearly how tasks are interconnected, whereas Gantt charts show the tasks against a calendar. The question of which to use is largely one of personal preference.

Software can be used to create project schedules but will only be as good as the information put into it.

Further reading

Tony Buzan: *How to Mind Map – The ultimate thinking tool that will change your life*, HarperCollins. ISBN: 0007146841

Alan Lawrie: *The Complete Guide to Creating and Managing New Projects for Voluntary Organisations*, Directory of Social Change. ISBN: 1903991153

CHAPTER THREE

Marketing and promotion

Marketing is the means by which a supplier of goods or services communicates messages to potential purchasers or consumers. For most industries this is fairly straightforward (though far from easy!) and the 'marketing mix' may include advertising, promotions, testimonials, direct selling and media coverage to name but a few. In the world of grant-funded projects, the role of marketing is perhaps less obvious. Rarely is there a product to sell, in the traditional sense, but instead there may be a need to attract people to take up a service or a course, or to raise awareness about a project locally or even nationally.

Everyone wants their projects to be successful and for most of us this means recruiting enough people to take part in project activities throughout the project's life. Recruitment of beneficiaries is vital to achieving project aims and yet many projects are only able to draw down part of their allocated funding because they have failed to recruit. Other projects don't have the same need to recruit beneficiaries, but have other marketing needs instead such as the need to publicise their work to gain support or funding.

This chapter looks at all aspects of marketing a project, from getting the initial offer right for the beneficiaries to planning a marketing campaign. Some of the more common marketing methods are looked at in detail, in some cases with discussion about their impact on the project as a whole. Finally, the chapter takes a look at the wider aspects of project promotion.

Every project is different and the needs, preferences, likes and dislikes of those at whom the project is aimed will vary widely. Rather than working through one case study, this chapter draws on a number of examples from real projects to illustrate good practice in marketing and promoting project activities

Recruiting beneficiaries

Those who are fairly new to running grant-funded projects may wonder about the purpose of this chapter. After all, how difficult can it be to 'sell' a free or highly subsidised product or service? Surely people will be queuing up to take advantage of this amazing offer? Well as anyone who has been around such projects for a while will know, it's perfectly possible to design a wonderful project, send out thousands of leaflets and get virtually no response. Why does this happen? There may be a number of reasons, and it's worth looking right through the process of attracting and recruiting people to take part in a project to see where the problem may lie.

Is the offer right? First things first – is what you're offering right for the people it's aimed at? A project needs to be:

- ■ Attractive
- ■ Helpful
- ■ Accessible.

If it fails on any of these three counts then any attempts at marketing are likely to fail. The key to getting the offer right is to have a genuine understanding of the people you are trying to target through the project – the project's beneficiaries. This is why grass roots voluntary and community sector organisations can sometimes have more success in recruiting beneficiaries than larger public sector organisations. It isn't that their marketing techniques are necessarily any better, but they are able to design the project so that it exactly meets the needs of the beneficiaries.

If you yourselves as the project team have a different kind of background than those you seek to help then it is advisable to seek the views and input of someone who does represent the potential beneficiaries to make sure that the project is going to be attractive. This can be done through research (see Chapter 1) or by getting their input in the design of the project.

Case Study – Leaving Care Project

A university wanted to design a resource pack, including a CD-ROM, for young people leaving care to help them make decisions and choices about their future education and careers. They formed a working group that included four young people who were in care, or had recently left care, to help design the CD-ROM and to advise on the content. As a result of the members of the working group, the CD-ROM was popular with young people leaving care, and they found it gave them the information and advice they needed.

As well as being **attractive**, the project offer has to be **helpful** to the beneficiary group. Sounds obvious doesn't it, especially as you have set out to help the beneficiaries in the first place. This is where the difference between a superficial and a deep understanding of the beneficiary group becomes obvious.

Case Study – Return to Work

A training provider designed a project aimed at lone parents to help them get back into work. The project offered a year-long part time diploma in a number of different subject areas, and provided full childcare and travel costs. The project proved to be attractive and hundreds of enquiries were received. However, after the first year only fourteen people out of a target of forty had signed up to the project, and five of these fourteen had dropped out. The project team commissioned an evaluation to work out why the project was not recruiting. The evaluators found that:

■ Many lone parents they talked to wanted to start with a shorter course to build their confidence and 'test the waters'. Signing up for a year-long course seemed too daunting and raised concerns about spending that much time away from their children.

■ Quite a number of the lone parents already had qualifications but needed to build their confidence and work experience instead.

■ Where further training was needed, this tended to be in highly specific areas. Up-to-date IT skills was the most commonly requested.

■ Some people questioned the diplomas on offer, as they felt they were not very well known by employers.

■ Most lone parents interviewed said they needed help with job search and CV writing, which was not offered by the project.

After the evaluation, the project manager said 'we had read lots of research suggesting that lone parents lack up to date qualifications, and when we carried out a small survey, the lone parents we contacted told us that the biggest barriers to learning were childcare and travel. We thought that by offering training combined with childcare and travel costs we'd be giving people exactly what they wanted. Perhaps when we did our survey we were asking the wrong questions!'

The above example shows that a project which seems right on the surface can be missing some vital ingredients that will attract beneficiaries. Lone parents in the area had initially shown interest because of the opportunities for free learning combined with childcare, but on learning more they were put off because they felt the project was too big a commitment of time and wouldn't meet their needs.

Finally, the project needs to be accessible to beneficiaries. There are obvious things that can be done to ensure that as many people as possible can benefit from a project – provision of transport or transport costs, provision of childcare and ensuring premises are adapted for wheelchair users are perhaps the most common measures taken. However, again a deep understanding of the needs of the beneficiary group will prevent assumptions being made that may turn out to be wrong.

Case Study – Rural Training Project

A training provider had run several successful projects in Wellasea, a medium sized coastal town, and wanted to expand its offer by running a training project for returners to the labour market from the many small rural villages and market towns in the district. As they had done in the past, they put on their training courses from 9.30a.m. – 3.00p.m. so that parents were able to drop off their children before attending. Because of their success in the past, the project team was expecting the take-up to be high. They were surprised to find that they hardly recruited anyone to the project and had to cancel several of the courses.

The team took a second look at their marketing strategy and redesigned the advertising leaflet. They made links with local community centres, job centres and careers advice centres to help get the word out about the project. Recruitment picked up a little, but not much.

Finally, the project manager happened to talk to the deputy head of a small primary school in one of the villages, who gave her the following advice:

'Most of the people you're targeting have children in primary school, and this could be your problem. Even though your catchment area is all within 20 miles of Wellasea, the small roads on the moors and traffic problems in Wellasea mean that most people are between 45 minutes and 1 hour away from your training centre. This is a problem for parents because most of the rural schools are so small that they don't actually have school gates. Parents have to drop their children off and wait with them until the

▶

school opens, which could be as late as 8.55a.m. – and there really isn't any wrap-around childcare available in most of the area. This means, of course, that most people wouldn't be able to get to Wellasea until after 9.30a.m.

'Just to make things more complicated, it's harvest time for many of the major local crops at the moment, so if you are targeting people from farming communities you are going to have a problem.'

The project manager immediately invited the deputy head to join the project's steering group! Based on this advice, the team redesigned the project so that there were more but shorter training sessions starting at 10.30a.m. They postponed all future courses until after the harvest, and in the end put the project on hold until the spring because some of the moor roads became impassable during the winter. In partnership with a number of local schools, they discussed running some courses more locally. This made the project more expensive because group size tended to be smaller, but along with the other changes it enabled the project to succeed when it had previously been failing.

The above example shows that issues of accessibility can go beyond the obvious, and that whereas project teams may think they are fitting the project around the beneficiaries (in this case, starting the course at 9.30a.m.) they might have missed something. The project manager was genuinely surprised to find that even a 9.30a.m. start time didn't allow parents to get there on time, but once armed with this knowledge was able to make changes that let the project succeed. Accessibility is discussed in greater detail in Chapter 5.

It is often the case that barriers to taking part in a project are psychological, even if practical reasons are given. Engaging with a project can be difficult for individuals for a variety of reasons. They may not be familiar with the organisation running the project and therefore have an unrealistic view of what the project will be like, especially if the organisation is seen as 'high status', such as a university or college. They may worry about fitting in with other participants. They may wonder if it really is for them, or whether people will look down upon them for 'asking for help'. If the project offers training, they may worry that they will do badly or reveal their lack of knowledge and be ridiculed or shouted at.

Case Study – Stanshall Estate

Redroof College had its main campus next door to Stanshall Estate, a large area of local authority housing within a fairly affluent town. While recruitment to college courses was good, it was rare for anyone from the Stanshall Estate to enrol. The community outreach team ran a short research project in which they sent questionnaires round to all the houses on the estate asking people which kinds of course they would be interested in doing, and to identify what their current barriers to participation were, from a list including:

- Childcare

- Finance

- Time

- Lack of previous qualifications.

Based on the results of the questionnaire, the college put on a series of free courses on IT and provided childcare. They stressed that no previous qualifications were necessary. They were surprised to find that these courses recruited very badly.

They asked a local voluntary sector organisation, Stanshall Voice, to carry out some research about why the project had failed so badly. Stanshall Voice trained up a number of local people to act as community researchers and to find out people's views on Redroof College and about learning in general. They were able to feed back the following findings:

- Most people felt intimidated about walking through the doors of the College. The College had recently fitted metal detectors and carried out bag searches, and this was felt to be too intrusive. Some people had actually gone along to courses only to turn back when faced by the search and by the 'unfriendly' receptionists

- The College was seen as a place for young people

- Many people reported 'I'm not the sort of person who goes to college'

- A lot of those interviewed had had bad experiences at school and feared that college would be the same. One woman said 'I couldn't be doing with someone going on at me for not doing my homework or whatever, not at my age.'

On the other hand, the researchers found that:

- Many mothers, and some fathers, were keen to learn more because they wanted to be able to support their children's learning and act as a positive role model

- Those few who had attended courses at the College were fiercely proud of being college students

- People were interested in a wide range of fairly ambitious topics such as local and family history, forensic science, criminology, digital photography and law as well as IT and basic skills.

As a result of the research, the team at Redroof College started to put on training courses in the Stanshall Community Centre, with a guided tour of the College part way through and one or more final sessions in the College building. The College also worked with a local university to put on taster days for some of the more popular course choices, either leading directly on to the course or on to appropriate access courses. Again, the taster days were run in the Community Centre and the courses ran their first few sessions there.

The above example demonstrates the importance of understanding not only the practical but also the psychological issues that might be deterring people from coming along to a project. The same is true for all projects, not just those offering learning. For example, an advice service may suffer from the same problems if the building and staff are seen to be too remote or unfriendly. Working with people from the groups or communities you hope to target and getting their formal input is a useful way to get closer to these issues, as well as empowering members of the community.

Once you are sure that the project is right, the next step is to ensure that enough potential beneficiaries get to hear about it. A number of factors are involved here. Who your beneficiaries are will be a major factor of course, but just as important is who you are as an organisation, and in particular the depth and breadth of your existing contact with the target group. Take for example a women's refuge that wants to run a confidence-building project. The refuge already has close links with the women it seeks to help, indeed most of them will come through the doors of their own accord.

Marketing for their project will therefore be a question of letting the women know that the project exists and how it might help them. Compare this with a training organisation that wants to run an IT support project for small businesses. The organisation may have few, if any, existing links with small businesses and will have to find a way to contact them and persuade them that the project could be useful. This is where a more systematic approach to marketing comes in useful.

Developing a marketing plan

A **marketing plan** brings together a number of different marketing methods and combines them to bring about the intended outcome – the recruitment of beneficiaries to the project. The ability to employ a variety of methods and to tailor them to the project and to the potential beneficiaries is crucial to a consistent level of success in marketing.

When developing the marketing plan the first place to start is to consider **who** your potential beneficiaries are. Do they form a distinct group or are the parameters a little more flexible? Are there particular characteristics that the beneficiaries will need in order to be eligible for support by the funding, for example do they need to be unemployed or to have a disability?

Secondly, you will need to think about how to reach your potential beneficiaries. Can you identify where they might naturally congregate, an essential service they might use on a regular basis, the newspapers and magazines they might read? All these are potential places for presenting a message.

Now you can start to think about how you will present the message and in what format. There are many ways to do this:

Method	Advantages	Disadvantages	Variations
Mailshot of leaflets	Well suited to projects targeting businesses or other organisations. Reaches a large number of people for relatively little effort. Can convey a lot of information.	May not be read. May not reach the right person within an organisation. 'Hit rate' will be low Database could be expensive and may not be up to date	Mailshots can be sent by fax or email instead. Postcards can be sent instead of leaflets. Individualised letters may be more effective in some cases.
Advert in local media	Good for reaching a wide range of people. Likely to generate lots of enquiries.	May need to set up an enquiry phone line for maximum impact and this can be resource intensive.	Advert in specialist publications likely to be read by potential beneficiaries. Press release. Advert on local radio.
Posters or leaflet drops	Can be put up in places potential beneficiaries are likely to go – schools, nurseries, community centres. Fairly inexpensive.	Easily ignored or overlooked.	Banner adverts on public transport.
Direct contact by phone or in person	Suited to some projects and beneficiary groups, especially where there is an existing relationship. Likely to be very effective.	'Cold calling' can be difficult to do. Can be time consuming.	Stall in high street, at conference, exhibition, trade fair, open day etc. Ask previous beneficiaries to act as 'ambassadors' for the project.

Rather than just relying on one method of marketing it is wise to combine a number of methods, especially if the project has high recruitment targets. The use of a variety of methods all working together makes the marketing effort much more effective, and really does mark out those who have put time into planning from those who have been more haphazard in their approach.

Case Study – Carers' Project

A community organisation wanted to run a project to support people with caring responsibilities in their local community. They had already worked with twelve carers and decided to contact them by phone or in person to see if they were interested in the new project.

They had a target of reaching twenty-five people in total and so looked at other ways to promote the project:

■ The people they were aiming to reach were quite likely to visit the doctor on a regular basis with those they were caring for, especially those caring for the elderly, so they decided to put up posters and leave leaflets in all the local surgeries.

■ Because the project covered quite a small geographic area they decided it would be cost effective to run a small advert in the local free newspaper.

■ The project team knew that there was a small but significant number of young people acting as carers in the area, so they contacted local secondary schools for help in identifying and reaching young carers.

Just as important as what will be done is when it will be done. A marketing plan should schedule the different marketing actions, so it will feed into the project plan. It will also involve costing up the marketing activities and therefore will also help with the development of the project budget.

In our example above, once the project team had decided on their marketing actions they were able to break this down into tasks for the project schedule:

Case Study Example – Schedule of Marketing Tasks for the Carers' Project

Task #	Task name	Duration (days)	Dependencies
01	Design posters	0.5	
02	Design leaflets	0.5	
03	Print leaflets and posters	10	01,02
04	Design newspaper advert	0.5	
05	Newspaper advert appears (milestone)	0	04
06	Contact doctors' surgeries	3	03
07	Take posters round to doctors'	2	03,06
08	Contact and have meetings with local schools	5	
09	Take enquiries by phone	15	05,07,08

Because this has an impact on the project schedule and costings, the ideal time to develop a marketing plan would be at the project planning stage before the bid or proposal was even written. However, this is unlikely to happen in practice because there is usually so much to do at this stage and so little time. A more pragmatic way would be to have an outline idea of the marketing plan and a total cost in mind, and develop this more fully once the project has started. If you do this, do remember to build in enough time to develop the marketing plan.

Designing written materials

Leaflets, posters, flyers, postcards – these are the staple marketing materials for many projects. They can be as elaborate as a full colour brochure or as simple as a hand-drawn poster, but the principles of communication remain the same. The material has to convey the benefits of the project to those it seeks to attract in a way that will persuade them that they would like to take part.

The most important consideration when designing written materials is to bear the audience in mind. You may be targeting a very tightly defined group of people or a wider section of the community, but in all cases the question to ask is, 'what is of interest to this group of people'. It's a common mistake to design materials that appeal to you and your colleagues but are much less appealing to the target group of beneficiaries. Key considerations include:

■ **Length.** Most people scan a leaflet or poster rather than reading it in full (unless they are very bored!) so you may only have a few seconds to catch their attention. Lengthy paragraphs of information will often not be read.

■ **Focus.** You, or more likely your bosses, may wish to include lengthy information about your organisation, but is this really what motivates your target group? When reading marketing material, most people want to know what is in it for them. Why would they want to take part in the project? What benefits will it bring them? How will it help them address their current concerns and problems? Everything else, other than basic factual information such as dates, times and contact details, is quite possibly irrelevant to the intended readers.

■ **Language.** The words we use tend to be a product of our background, upbringing and profession, and different groups of people use language very differently. Is the language used on your marketing materials appropriate to and understandable by the target group? A word of caution on this, however. There can be a fine line between using appropriate language and sounding patronising, or even plain stupid! Think about middle aged adults trying to talk like teenagers, for example. There are some basic things you can do to make your marketing materials more understandable though, such as avoiding jargon and using straightforward language. If the people you are targeting do not have English as their first language then you might want to consider translating the materials, but be aware of raising false expectations if your project is to be conducted entirely in English.

■ **Layout.** This should be appealing, but beyond this it should organise the information so that it is easily taken in and digested. Use of headings, bullet points and highlighting key words can all help, as can the appropriate use of colour to draw attention to the main information. Just as important as the presentation is how the content is organised. This should follow some kind of logical order, drawing attention to the main points early on and filling these out with more information once the reader's attention has been caught.

Diagrams, artwork and photographs can add interest to marketing materials and draw people's attention in a way that text alone is not able to do. It is said that a picture is worth a thousand words, but you need to make sure that these are the right words. Sometimes a picture can have connotations that are not immediately obvious but which nonetheless can have a big impact on successful marketing. A simple example is a project aimed at people from the Bangladeshi community that has a photograph in its leaflet showing white and black African people taking part in project activities. Such a picture might say, 'this project isn't really for you', or even worse, 'we don't really know the difference between different ethnic minority communities'. It's perhaps worth running a proposed picture past a few different people and asking them what it says to them before including it in marketing material.

Marketing through direct contact

Direct contact with potential beneficiaries can be the most powerful way of letting people know about the project and of drawing in those people who may not be reached by other marketing methods. While mailshots can be enormously effective, especially if the project is well designed and is offering something of immediate interest, it can sometimes be a hit and miss affair. The written word can be very effective at getting across the main points of the project, but it can't answer questions such as 'is it for me?' or 'will I fit in?' that could be at the forefront of people's minds. The nature of many grant-funded projects, especially those aimed at individuals rather than businesses, means that the people being targeted may well lack confidence. There is also the issue of trust to consider. If the organisation offering the project is not well known to someone, they may feel uncertain or even suspicious about what is on offer. On the other hand, hearing about the project from a trusted person can be reassuring. It also allows the potential beneficiary to discuss the project over a period of time, to learn more about it and consider how it might help them and how they can overcome any barriers that might be preventing them from taking part.

Not every organisation that runs a project will have that level of existing contact with potential beneficiaries to be able to market on a one-to-one basis, and of course it won't always be necessary or practical to do so. For projects that are trying to work with 'hard to reach' groups, and especially people who may be lacking in confidence, it may be useful. There are a number of different approaches that can be used, for example:

- Partnering with another organisation that works more closely with the potential beneficiary group

- Employing outreach workers

- Employing people who have been successfully helped by previous projects to carry out outreach work

- Using other marketing methods, such as posters or leaflets, but following this up with a high level of one to one contact

- Offering initial advice as an integral part of the project, providing you have suitably trained advice and guidance staff.

As well as being an effective method of attracting people to the project in the first place, a high level of one to one support throughout the project can also be important in ensuring that people stay with the project rather than dropping out. Taking part in a grant-funded project tends to be something that people do at a point of change in their lives. Taking a training or education course, returning to work, addressing life problems and issues, joining a social or sports group – all these things can have a huge impact on individual lives, and this process of change can at times be disconcerting. Having someone to turn to for advice or just a chat can ease the process enormously and provide much needed reassurance that the change will not be overwhelming. And by the way, it is easy to overestimate the resilience of individuals who are taking part in a project. A senior manager can be just as unsettled by executive training as a small child by starting school! Fear of change is part of the human condition and none of us is immune. Having the right support in place can be an essential component of the project.

Referral partners

Partnering up with an organisation that is close to the potential beneficiary group was suggested above as one way of carrying out face to face marketing of the project. This can be taken a step further by developing a network of referral partners who work in some capacity with potential beneficiaries and are willing to promote the project to them.

This sounds like a very simple idea and indeed it is, but be warned it takes a huge amount of time and effort to set up a good system of referrals. Once established, however, this can quickly become the main method of marketing for an organisation. Perhaps more importantly, it provides for a more coherent service for the beneficiaries. Using a network of referrals establishes that all partners are working together to provide a set of helpful services, rather than working competitively against each other to get 'bums on seats' and hence funding.

A referral partner can be anyone who works with your target group on a regular basis – Jobcentre Plus, doctors, schools, chambers of commerce, trades unions, advice and guidance workers, social workers and so on. Your first task, having established a contact with a potential referral partner, will be to demonstrate to them that your project will be of genuine benefit to their clients. After all, they are unlikely to refer anyone to you if they are in any way unsure that the project will be in their clients' best interests. Once you have crossed this bridge, the next stage is to ensure that as many individuals as possible within the partner organisation are made aware of and fully understand the project. This might involve giving a presentation or sending out clear and concise written materials.

Just providing a general contact number will not usually be enough, especially if you are working with partners who work quite intensively with people, such as social workers or advice and guidance workers. They will want to be able to get in touch with a named contact and know that their referral will be followed up promptly so that their client is not left unsupported. This is why it will be important to ensure that a named person or their nominated deputy is available within your organisation at all times to take referrals and is prepared to follow these up by contacting the potential beneficiary by phone or in person within a set time. It is also advisable to feed back to the referring organisation to let them know whether or not their client was offered a place on the project and whether they took it up or not.

Following these good practice points will ensure that referral partners become partners in more than name only. For more detail on partnership working, please see Chapter 5.

Case Study – Highby Grove Community Centre

Highby Grove Community Centre runs a project called 'Community Heart' which aims to reach out to those suffering from ill health, isolation and other social problems, offering a programme of activities in a sociable environment. Over the seven years since it was set up, the Centre manager has set up working referral mechanisms with:

- The local NHS Primary Care Trust, and individual doctors' surgeries

- Social Services

- 'Celebrate', a local mental health charity

- The local branch of Help the Aged.

The manager meets with staff in the partner organisations every three months for a general update on the project and to discuss any issues arising out of the partnership. All referrals are made to the Centre Manager by telephone, email or post and are followed up within three working days. The manager or her deputy aim to meet with people who are referred to the project face to face, but where this is not possible they will telephone and arrange a meeting at a later date. The manager always reports back on the progress of referred beneficiaries at the regular partner meetings.

As a result of this successful network of referral partners, the project does not carry out any other marketing activities other than posting general project information on the notice board outside the Community Centre.

How can you keep in touch? If your organisation is planning to run a number of projects over a period of time it will certainly be worth keeping in touch with people you have worked with and supported in previous projects. Not only are people likely to come back and participate in future projects, but keeping your organisation at the forefront of their minds is likely to result in greater word-of-mouth marketing. A simple newsletter, either printed or emailed, allows you to keep people in touch with new projects and opportunities from you or your partner organisations. As well as using such a newsletter as a marketing opportunity, it will be worth investing a little time in gathering articles and information to include as well, otherwise it could start to look like one big advert.

Publicising a successful project

Sometimes, telling potential beneficiaries about the project is not enough, the rest of the world needs to know as well. Gaining publicity for the project, either as it starts up or to celebrate its success, might be something you need to do to help gain further funding or to gain publicity for your organisation. It might also be about ensuring that your local community knows about you and the services you provide.

Press releases are a quick way of getting the message out via the media. Where possible it is advisable to use your professional marketing staff, or those of a partner organisation, as they are likely to have good existing links with the media and extensive experience of writing press releases. However it is possible to write your own press release if necessary.

First of all, as with marketing in general, it is important to consider the audience. In this case the audience is likely to be fairly wide, but you may need to think about the style and tone of the publication (or radio or TV station) that you are targeting. What kind of story do they tend to publish and what angle do they prefer? Newspapers (especially national ones) are inundated with press releases, so you need to ensure that what you write is capable of catching their interest.

Secondly, you will need to take a good hard look at what is likely to be 'newsworthy' about your project. It is likely that you are too close to the project to be objective about it, especially if you have been working on it for some time, so it is worth discussing your ideas with someone who has been less involved. In any case, you will need to present a particular angle on the story by emphasising, for example, a particular aspect such as a case study or the impact on the community.

This angle on the story needs to be emphasised in the first paragraph of your press release. The rest of the release should fill in the essential information needed to put this first paragraph into context. This is often known as the 'five W's' – what, where, when, who and why. It is important to stick to basic factual information here, though one or more quotes from those directly involved in the news story are generally included. The style should be simple and direct, and it is usual to write press releases in the third person.

Any additional background information such as information about the organisation involved is usually included at the end of the press release.

Finally, make sure you start the press release with a good, punchy title. Again, this should emphasise your particular angle on the story. Think 'headline' here, though the publication may well develop their own headline instead. Try and keep the title simple and factual though, rather than trying to develop a clever or jokey headline.

When presenting the press release, use one side of the paper only, double space typing and keep it shorter than 2 sides of A4. A standard format would be:

- Write 'Press Release' or 'News Release' at the top of the page
- Include the date
- Include your name, title and contact details (or put these at the end)
- Title
- Initial sentence or two that sums up the story
- Further paragraphs that answer 'what, where, when, who and why'
- Relevant quotes
- If you go to a second page, write 'more' at the foot of the first page
- At the end of the main body of the text, write 'ends'
- Include a 'Notes for Editors' section which gives further information such as details about your organisation and perhaps information about the funding scheme. These details are often presented as a bullet pointed or numbered list.

Dissemination conferences are often held at the end of a project to communicate what has been done and what has been learned. In planning a dissemination conference it is important to bear in mind:

■ **The audience.** Who do you want to present the message to? Your invited audience could include senior representatives of partner organisations, potential future funders, local dignitaries such as Councillors and MPs, or any particular target group that you feel should know more about the project, e.g. parents, the elderly, children. A common mistake of dissemination events is 'preaching to the converted', as only those who already know about and are engaged with the project turn up.

■ **Key messages.** What do people need to know and why? Whether you are seeking further funding, informing potential beneficiaries or trying to raise the profile of your organisation within the local community, find your point and stick to it. People may be quickly turned off by lengthy presentations about the history of the project or speeches by invited guests who appear not to know much about the project at all.

■ **Celebrate success.** If the project has been successful you should give due recognition to those who have helped make it so, including any beneficiaries who have perhaps put in an enormous effort themselves in taking part in the project.

■ **Make the event accessible.** Do remember to hold your conference at a time and location that will suit your invited audience.

Publicity events can take many forms depending on the nature of the project. Performance events, dinners, events in public spaces such as shopping malls and a range of more imaginative publicity stunts can all be used to raise the profile of your project and/or organisation. The only limits are imagination and the law!

Summary

Whether you need to recruit beneficiaries to your project or to raise its profile more generally, a structured approach to marketing can help.

What your project offers to beneficiaries should be **attractive**, **helpful** and **accessible** in order to maximise the number of people who want to and are able to take up the offer.

Barriers to participating in a project may be practical, psychological or a combination of the two. A deep understanding of the needs of your target beneficiary group is invaluable in ensuring that the project genuinely meets their needs.

A **marketing plan** brings together a number of different marketing methods in combination and schedules the tasks necessary to carry them out. When creating a marketing plan it is important to think carefully about the target beneficiary group in order to find the best methods to reach them with your message.

Written marketing materials should be developed with the audience in mind and be written in a way that is interesting and appealing to them. Key considerations are **length**, **focus**, **language** and **layout**. If including pictures, consider carefully the message they convey.

Direct contact with beneficiaries is a very powerful way of marketing as it allows potential beneficiaries to discuss their hopes and fears. Where direct contact is not possible, **referral partners** can be developed. A system of referrals takes time and effort to set up but can be an excellent marketing method.

Methods of creating general publicity for your projects include **press releases**, **dissemination conferences** and **publicity events**. Press releases are a quick way of getting a story out to the media. Dissemination conferences are often held at the end of a project to publicise its results. There is a wide range of other publicity events that can be tried both during and after the project.

Further reading

Much of the information presented in this chapter is not explicitly covered in any marketing literature. However, the Voluntary Arts Network has an excellent section on its website about marketing and publicity that is relevant to a wide range of organisations in all sectors. It can be found at: www.voluntaryarts.org under the "running your group" link.

CHAPTER FOUR

Equality, diversity and inclusion

equality   the state or an instance of being equal; especially, the state of enjoying equal rights in political, economic or social affairs.[1]

diversity   the range of visible and non-visible differences that exist between people.[2]

inclusion   in equal opportunities terms is about making every member of a community feel that they are not prevented from taking part in any activity,...because of any personal characteristic relating to their race or ethnicity, sex, disability status, sexual orientation, religion or belief, class or age.[3]

Short definitions such as those above are a useful starting point for the exploration of most fields or issues. They are, though, just that: starting points. They give us a clue but usually leave many more questions to be answered.

The dictionary definition of equality above refers quite quickly to 'equal rights', which points us immediately to the law. Campaigns for, and struggles over, 'equal rights' have a very long history indeed in many countries. In the UK, 'common law' protects our rights. We can also now appeal to laws of the European Union. We have also a range of laws concerned specifically with preventing discrimination, promoting equality of opportunity and good relations between different groups.

Clearly, this legal framework is critical for project designers and managers. Apart from anything else the law places requirements on us all. You could be held personally accountable if a case of discrimination were brought by someone against your project. However, legal compliance is really only the starting point. Often more challenging is meeting the general public expectations which now exist around best practice for equality, diversity and inclusion.

This chapter takes an overview of the background, policy and practice of equality, diversity and inclusion as it relates to project management.

---

1   *Reader's Digest Universal Dictionary*, 1989
2   Kandola, R and Fullerton, J, 1998 *Diversity in Action: Managing the Mosaic* (2nd Edition), Institute of Personnel and Development
3   AUA (with ECU and HEEON)(2005) *A-Z Equality & Diversity*

Equality of treatment and avoiding unfair discrimination

This is the approach to equality which has the longest history in UK legislation and is probably now most familiar to us. It has underpinned policies across the public, private and voluntary sectors for almost forty years. Over this time, the approach has created a large number of jobs, required very significant public expenditure to ensure compliance with the law, led to the development of a significant infrastructure to support organisations in implementing the legal framework (for example bodies such as The Commission for Racial Equality, the Equality Challenge Unit and the Equal Opportunities Commission), and provided a market for books such as the present one. Some have argued that what we have created is collectively little more than a self-serving and self-perpetuating 'equal opportunities industry'.

> 'I do not discriminate. I treat everyone exactly the same no matter who they are'.

Unfair discrimination occurs when a group or an individual is treated less or more favourably than others because factors are used to reach judgements about them which are unrelated to their ability or potential.

The idea that if we treat everyone in the same way then we will, by definition, avoid discriminating against anyone is common. Equal opportunity policies and practices are built partly on this idea.

The procedures, policies and practices of any organisation, and project, should be fair and should not discriminate against, or favour, some groups or individuals because of their personal characteristics or position. For example, if the project policy is that staff should be appraised formally each year then this should be applied equally to all. In the same way, the criteria for allocating funding to different aspects of the project should be such that they do not favour some groups or individuals over others just because of who they are.

However, treating everyone the same in terms of ensuring rules and procedures are fair should not be confused with the idea that everyone is actually the same. We are not all the same and – notwithstanding our rights in law – we are not all equal in terms of our access to various resources and opportunities which affect our life chances.

Although we are all individuals, certain physical, cultural and behavioural characteristics come to be given particular meaning or significance in any society or culture. These characteristics are said to be socially constructed.

A project designer and/or manager has to acknowledge, in practices and policies, the complex relationship between individual and socially constructed 'difference' in order to promote equality as opportunity.

Case Study – Job Interviewing

The project manager and her team decide on the questions they will ask candidates for the job as project officer, related to the published job description and person specification for the post. The interview panel have agreed to ask all candidates exactly the same questions.

The ability to be flexible about working hours is important in the project design. There could be some essential evening work and/or some early morning starts for meetings or other essential tasks. There could even be the occasional weekend work. This feature of the work was signalled in the advertisement and further particulars for the post.

The agreement is to ask each candidate to confirm their ability to be flexible in terms of working hours. However, during the interviews the project director decides to pursue with two female candidates only their domestic commitments and whether this flexibility is actually possible for them, despite them stating clearly that it is.

Here we have an all too typical situation. On paper, the project and its team is attempting to follow standard 'equality of opportunity' practice in selection processes. They are, for example, restricting their questioning to the job and person specification and treating every candidate the same in terms of the schedule of questions – in other words they are creating 'fair rules of the game'. On the other hand, we have an individual – possibly influential in the decision-making process through his position – who is treating two candidates differently from other candidates on the grounds of their perceived similarity to each other.

This is an example of direct discrimination.

Direct discrimination occurs when factors unrelated to the ability or merit of a group or individual are used explicitly or directly as a reason for discriminating against them. For example, not recruiting someone with a disability even though they are more appropriately qualified for the job than the person appointed, simply because the candidate has a disability.

The project director in our case study probably sees his behaviour as being reasonable, sensible and even fair. He is 'acknowledging difference'. The problem with uncritically accepting 'socially constructed differences' is that it leads to stereotyping.

Stereotyping is the process of applying to individuals the characteristics of the group to which the individual is perceived to belong. It can result in positive or negative outcomes for the individual(s) concerned and it happens whenever generalisations are made about people. The main problem with stereotyping is when it leads to prejudging individuals and/or making assumptions about them. This can lead easily to discriminatory actions.

Stereotyping therefore ignores the multitude of different ways in which people who share a particular background, circumstance, physical or cultural characteristic interpret it and therefore also ignores the many and varied ways in which it does and doesn't impact on them and their behaviour.

For example, whilst we know that Islam expresses particular views about drinking alcohol it is the case that individual Muslims in the UK (and elsewhere) interpret what their religion says about alcohol consumption in differing ways in their daily lives. Similarly, individuals with the same physical disability will deal with it differently in their daily lives as will those with caring responsibilities.

Acknowledging differences between individuals is essential to good equal opportunities practice, but it must not be based on imagined or stereotyped group characteristics.

So, in the case study above, the questioning of the two female candidates should not assume that flexible working is necessarily a problem for these candidates. In any event, the way in which the job is designed, organised and managed should be such that a candidate with caring responsibilities is still able to do the job, if they are considered the best person for it. If this is not the case, then we may be indirectly discriminating.

Indirect discrimination occurs when regulations, procedures and policies have a negative discriminatory effect on certain groups compared to others.

It is important to stress at this point that UK legislation relating to race and ethnic relations, sex discrimination, and disability discrimination considers that intentions or motives are not relevant, in the law, to demonstrating that direct or indirect discrimination has taken place. Whilst you may not have intended to unfairly discriminate (either personally or through the rules and procedures of your project) the law focuses on the outcomes or effects of policies and practices not your intentions.

The main lesson from the job interviewing case study is that treating everyone the same in terms of 'the rules of the game' may be good equal opportunities practice but we must also acknowledge difference to ensure an 'equal playing field'.

Action checklist

■ Avoid stereotyping by **consciously** questioning whether your plans and practices involve generalisations about groups or communities.

■ Create fair 'rules of the game' by **consciously** checking that everyone can play by them irrespective of their circumstances or individual characteristics.

■ Acknowledge difference **consciously** in order to ensure a 'level playing field' by ensuring there are no unnecessary barriers to anyone with the appropriate ability from participating.

Try to apply these broad principles to the following case study. The following questions may help to guide your thinking.

1. What are the issues for anti-discriminatory practice revealed by this example? Consider both direct and indirect discrimination.

2. What would you do differently, if anything?

3. What might be the challenges you would have to resolve in order to meet the principles of anti-discriminatory practice in this project design?

Case Study – Sport For All

This project was designed by a voluntary group to encourage young and older men and women who had not usually engaged in sporting activities to experience the benefits that sport can bring. It provided the opportunity to sample different sports, at beginner level, in supervised bite-size sessions offered on two weekday evenings and

on Saturday mornings. Participants had to self-certify that they had
no health problems that might make participation potentially
dangerous for them. The sessions were held at a sports centre and
included softball soccer, basketball and netball, tennis, swimming
and diving, bowls, croquet and roller skating.

The project team encountered two immediate difficulties resulting
from failure to consider what the name of their project implied and
their inability to deliver it. There were no childcare facilities in the
sports centre and the absence of this quickly meant that several
potential participants who were single parents realised they would
be unable to join the scheme. The project team then faced
questions from a potential participant who had quite severe sight
impairment. They realised that they did not have specialist
facilitators/supervisors to manage this appropriately and safely.

Evidence over many years shows clearly that people with certain social,
personal and/or cultural characteristics typically have reduced opportunities
compared to those who do not have these characteristics. This project is
perpetuating that pattern of inequality of opportunity by making
stereotypical assumptions about the target market for sporting activity.

To repeat our earlier discussion: the anti-discriminatory approach signals
that the project team has to consider how it can avoid unfairly
discriminating against these individuals. To do this the team must reflect
critically on the assumptions they are making, on the stereotypes with
which they may be (unconsciously) operating and consider ways in which
they can better acknowledge the different individual circumstances of
people who are – in this example – single parents and/or visually impaired.
Unless the team does this they could be guilty of unfair discrimination.

In this example, then, the team might consider:

- Re-thinking and re-designing the activities to make them safely
  accessible to people with certain disabilities, even without specialist
  disability support

- Hiring specialist coaching staff with experience of working with the
  disabled

- Some training for the core coaching staff in providing a safe and
  productive environment for people with disabilities

■ Providing child care facilities and/or re-thinking the timing of the sessions for example so that they take place during school hours.

You might reflect at this point on other ways the project team could **design out the potential for unfair discrimination**. Might there be other groups who could claim that they are unfairly discriminated against in this project?

Building the anti-discriminatory approach into the very first phase of project design is absolutely essential:

■ Because the law demands that we do

■ Because it can be very difficult (and very costly) indeed to 'reverse engineer' the project design and implementation strategy, once it is in place, in order to do so.

Positive action

This aspect of equality as opportunity practice highlights that there is much more that can be done to promote equal opportunities over and above avoiding various forms of unfair discrimination.

It demands *proactive* and *positive* policies and actions in addition to the necessary, but essentially, *reactive* and *defensive* tendency of the anti-discriminatory approach.

Positive action is an intervention strategy to reduce discrimination and/or to redress past patterns of inequality which were the result of discrimination or disadvantage. It is effectively about 'levelling the playing field'. It is not the same as **positive discrimination**. This would occur if someone or group was treated more favourably than others in the same situation solely on the basis of their group characteristic (e.g. their ethnicity or gender). This is unlawful in the UK except for the provision that it might be legitimate for certain jobs to be restricted to people from certain backgrounds or with particular characteristics. This is known as the GOR – Genuine Occupational Requirement. An example might be recruiting only from people of a particular sex for jobs involving particularly intimate personal care.

> ## Case Study – The Racial Equality Unit
>
> This project was established in a university, using government project funding, to promote increased access to the university for members of minority ethnic communities, both as students and staff, and to ensure their equal opportunities once they were part of the university community.
>
> Much of the work of unit staff was devoted to being proactive in engaging directly with these communities. These initiatives included, for example, producing course literature in key minority ethnic languages and distributing it via networks established with individuals and organisations within the minority communities; establishing facilities for religious worship on campus for those of various faiths and ensuring course timetabling allowed for this; working with minority ethnic students to create support networks.
>
> This strategy was based on the principle of positive action – reaching out proactively in targeted and specific ways to these communities and also then responding as positively as possible to the perspectives, experiences and needs of those groups through policy and practice development.

This grant-funded project was launched as long ago as the mid-1980s and finished as an identified project in the early 1990s. Innovative in its time, this type of positive action approach to 'equality as opportunity' is now firmly established as the basis for good practice.

It is important to recognise that this case study was not about positive discrimination. If it had been, this would have involved offering places to students on the grounds of their ethnic origin irrespective of their demonstrating the ability to benefit from higher education study. This was not the approach – and just as well since it is, as we have seen, unlawful.

Positive action strategies require that you ask yourself two basic questions.

■ Will the ways in which we are planning to do things – marketing, advertising, staff recruitment, location of activities and meetings, governance structures, etc – tend to reproduce involvement in our project mainly or only by those who typically engage with, and/or benefit from, such initiatives?

■ Are there ways in which we can reach out to groups, communities and individuals, as appropriate to our objectives, who do not tend to become involved with/benefit from such projects?

Positive action strategies can and should influence all elements of a project design and its management. However, this is not just an altruistic strategy. Positive action is a way in which you can really enhance the quality of your project.

Reaching out to individuals, groups and communities as beneficiaries of the project and/or as staff working on it – who may typically experience various forms of discrimination and/or disadvantage – widens the pool of experiences, skills and talents from which your project draws.

Action checklist

■ Examine project objectives to see if they are actively seeking to reach people who may typically not engage in your area of work or this type of project, either as target beneficiaries or as project employees.

■ If they are not doing this, then are there any legitimate reasons why not?

■ If you are actively pursuing positive action then all elements of the project will be informed by this. For example:

☐ Are you targeting your advertising appropriately?

☐ Are you using language in all your project materials that will resonate with, and appeal to, the target groups or communities?

☐ Have you appropriate staff training in place in order to ensure your strategy is understood and implemented 'on the ground' and not just on paper?

☐ Is appropriate funding set aside in your budget to support your positive action strategy?

■ Examine your monitoring and evaluation procedures to ensure they explicitly report on the success of, or difficulties with, the strategy.

Equality of outcomes

In the main, positive action falls short of aiming to uncover and then redress the reasons underlying patterns of previous disadvantage or inequality. This is consistent with its place in the 'equality of opportunity' perspective which emphasises, as we have seen, making sure the 'rules of the game' are fair and the field on which it is played is as level as possible.

'Equality of outcomes' is an interventionist approach which looks to redistribute resources to disadvantaged groups and communities. As the name implies, its success is normally measured by the extent to which the interventions mean that such groups do gain increased access to those resources which enhance life chances.

Case Study – Aimhigher

This national project is designed to increase and widen participation in universities and colleges by (mainly) 18 to 30-year-olds from areas or social backgrounds with below average higher education participation rates. It aims to do this through initiatives and actions with such groups to:

- Raise awareness of the benefits and opportunities HE study brings

- Raise aspirations towards HE study

- Raise achievement at school.

Organised on a regional and sub-regional basis across England and Wales, the overall target to which Aimhigher is meant to be a very significant contributor is that by 2010, 50% of the 18 to 30 population will have experienced some form of higher education study.

The national guidelines for regional and sub-regional project designers and managers provide very little guidance about actual interventions but they do make very clear the kinds of groups and individuals with whom projects are expected to engage. The overwhelming majority of the very significant funding available is targeted at the most (socially, educationally and economically) disadvantaged areas as measured by national statistical (and other reputable research) evidence.

The project at national level has established an impact and evaluation strategy involving measuring the effectiveness of various interventions at increasing and widening participation of the targeted groups.

If you compare the Racial Equality Unit and the Aimhigher case studies, it becomes perhaps easier to see how positive action underpins but differs from 'equality of outcome'. The approach of the university project was not to divert or target interventions at deep-rooted causes of low participation in higher education by members of minority ethnic communities. It did bring additional resources to bear on low participation but these were targeted and used to proactively and positively change the ways in which the university engaged with these communities. The project did not, for example, target additional resources at improving levels of attainment of school students in the minority ethnic communities – which could be said to be one factor in low participation by such young people in higher education.

Whilst clearly embracing the idea of positive action, the Aimhigher project is targeting resources explicitly to try and redress key factors in past and continuing patterns of educational inequality: For example, the project places extra and specialised human and other resources into schools in an explicit attempt to change deep-rooted socially and culturally established attitudes (aspirations) and behaviours (attainment) which we know affect participation in higher education study and the improved life chances it can bring.

This may sound like a very subtle difference between the two projects and in some ways it is. However, they have quite different practical implications for project designers and managers.

A project based on the 'equality of outcome' perspective will have a clear **interventionist strategy** which goes beyond positive action processes, and is designed to achieve fundamental changes to patterns of equality and inequality in the particular field. The project is likely to attempt to have an equal effect on different groups or communities.

The key issue you need to consider in designing and managing a project built on the principle of equality of outcome is that attempting to achieve the same outcomes for different groups means you must actively acknowledge, and fully take into account, the range and nature of these groups. You must embrace diversity and difference.

Diversity and difference

We have already seen that social differences, which can be highly individualised, must be acknowledged in your project procedures and processes as part of an 'equality of opportunity' approach. Such differences are acknowledged and lie at the heart of positive action strategies. The inequalities related to these socially constructed differences are the prime target of 'equality of outcome' approaches.

Diversity clearly involves difference. It implies multiformity as opposed to uniformity. It also recognises, upfront, that difference is not a neutral idea. In essence, there are two evaluative dimensions to the idea of 'being different'.

On the one hand, difference is often evaluated negatively in the sense of 'being different from some norm'. This can lead to those who are defined as 'different' being marginalised or excluded. Difference is an evaluative term. What this means in practice is that it involves power. Put simply, there are those with the power to influence what we define as the 'norm' against which difference is (negatively) evaluated.

On the other hand, difference can be evaluated as a cause for celebration because it enriches life (or a project) through bringing diversity. Here, the power of institutions and/or groups (or even individuals) to shape how we evaluate difference in relation to a norm is being challenged.

We have, actually, dealt with the first way in which difference can be interpreted. We saw it in the Sport For All case study. Although the second interpretation of difference might be said to inform the Racial Equality Unit case study it does so more implicitly than explicitly. What would a strategy look like which explicitly set out to celebrate difference and diversity?

The key elements of such a strategy would be:

- Aims, objectives and policies explicitly and proactively seek diversity

- An approach to management which celebrates and does not simply (or reluctantly) accept differences between individuals and groups

- Processes which proactively encourage differences (of culture, experiences, background, skill, knowledge, etc) to be explored and developed in productive ways.

It is not difficult to imagine that being able to draw on the widest range of relevant experiences, perspectives and skills is likely to enhance the ability of a project to meet its objectives – possibly more effectively and possibly more efficiently.

The important point to remember in this strategy is that it is not about diversity for its own sake. The emphasis here on (pro) actively recognising that individual, social and cultural differences can produce enormous benefits for your project brings with it an immediate contribution to redressing past and/or continuing patterns of inequality (see below). It achieves this by ensuring that those experiences, perspectives or abilities which might have been marginalised or excluded in the past are now positively evaluated.

Equally, however, this approach is neither about 'quotas' nor 'representation'.

Quotas and targets both involve setting a fixed proportion. Using **quotas** related to social characteristics (gender, ethnicity, age. class, for example) is a form of positive discrimination and is unlawful. For example, setting a quota that 30% of those working on a project will be women would imply that you will achieve this irrespective of any others factors such as the person's qualifications. Setting a **target** is different – and is lawful – because it could be achieved legitimately through positive action strategies and is an aim or ambition of the project not a requirement.

Representation is perhaps a little more complex. It typically has two aspects:

- ■ The so-called 'matching' principle
- ■ The notion of 'social representativeness'.

It can be argued that in some cases it is important and necessary that those leading and/or undertaking particular tasks or priorities in a project are from particular backgrounds. This is sometimes known as 'matching'.

For example, it has been argued that those working with minority ethnic groups and communities may be more likely to achieve objectives if they are also of that ethnicity. In some cases, as we have seen, 'matching' might be justified in terms of a 'GOR' but outside these rather narrow legal limits it can be more complex to implement as the case study below demonstrates.

Case Study – Research Project with Young Muslim Women

This project was designed, and funded, to explore the perspectives of young Muslim women (16 to 24) about the role which education plays in their individual thinking and planning for their future.

▶

▶

> The research project designers made it clear in their bid for funding
> that the field researcher who would undertake questionnaires and
> some in-depth interviews would be a young Muslim woman with an
> appropriate academic/research background in order to maximise the
> quality of the data gathered from the sample of respondents.
>
> The young female Muslim researcher appointed reported after about
> six months into the project that there were clear and (she believed)
> significant social and cultural differences between her and many of
> the target group. For example, she was used to wearing western
> dress (including make up) and this appeared to put up a barrier for
> some of the respondents (and especially the parents of the 16 to
> 18-year-olds for whom parental consent to participate was
> necessary) who were from very traditional Islamic communities here
> in the UK.

Matching is a complex and disputed strategy for project management. If
this seems an option worth considering for your project then ask yourself:

- Why is this a route worth considering?
- What am I trying to achieve with this strategy?
- Are there other ways I could ensure project workers are best able to
  achieve goals with the target groups or communities?
- What do members of those groups or communities themselves feel
  about those working with them?
- Is there any evidence from other projects that 'matching' is necessary
  or leads to greater effectiveness in this field of work?

The idea of social representativeness is similar to 'matching' but focuses
particularly on ensuring that decision-making bodies for your project (such
as a steering group or practitioner group) have a membership which is fully
representative of the groups or communities implicated in your project.
Although this is both sensible and appropriate, implementation is not
always that easy. This is because 'difference', as we have seen, is socially
constructed and involves differences of power between groups and
organisations.

Case Study – Project Steering Group

This project was concerned with assisting those who were under/unemployed to gain access to work experience (with supporting formal training) with Small & Medium-Sized Enterprises (SMEs). The overall objective was to not only provide improved chances for employment for the beneficiaries but to do so in ways which would directly benefit the participating SMEs. The project was designed to include 'live' project work by the beneficiary. The project was to be identified, and needed, by the SME.

The target SMEs would include a number whose business was aimed primarily at the needs of minority ethnic communities in the area/region. The project designer included in the indicative membership of the project steering group two members (out of eight) to be 'representatives of minority ethnic business and/or communities'.

What the project designers had not fully anticipated were the intense rivalries that existed between different minority ethnic communities in regard to their access to such positions of influence, and the equally (perhaps more) intense disagreements within and between minority ethnic communities in the area about the status of so-called 'community representatives' who often seemed to sit on such bodies.

What these examples remind us is that there are almost certainly as many things that differentiate people as *appear* to unite them.

Action checklist

■ Research, map and understand the *complexity of shared and simultaneously differentiated experiences and identities of the groups*, communities and partners with which you intend to work.

■ Research and understand the power relations between the groups and communities with which the project will be engaging.

■ Always involve the groups or communities directly in your efforts to fully understand the complexities and dynamics of their situations.

■ Get those groups and communities involved as early as possible in the genesis of the project design.

■ Be careful of taking short cuts using the most easily identifiable or known points of contact with particular groups or communities.

Once fully articulated, your strategy to celebrate diversity and difference will:

■ Proactively, explicitly and positively acknowledge that those typically or often excluded from, or marginalised in, access to important resources including power will add value to the project

■ Emphasise this positive contribution in real terms, through explicit objectives, targets and ways of working such as how you construct decision-making forums

■ Open up access and challenge existing patterns in the distribution of power and influence

■ Not oversimplify social, cultural and other differences between groups or communities but will acknowledge the complexities which come about through the social construction of difference

■ Challenge the 'deficit model' of 'disadvantaged' groups or communities which can be a tendency of some approaches to 'equality of opportunity' and even of some positive action strategies.

This may sound very positive and appealing but it does bring real challenges for the project designer and manager. These are, chiefly:

■ Creating a project culture and ethos which welcomes difference rather than uniformity and conformity

■ Ensuring sufficient resources to manage potentially very diverse group and/or individual requirements

■ Continuous efforts to transform potentially destructive conflict created by 'difference' into constructive, empowering and productive decision-making and action.

Inclusion

By now, given the structure of this chapter, you might anticipate that this section brings our journey through key elements of project management for equality, diversity and inclusion to a logical conclusion. You should have seen how anti-discriminatory approaches, though fundamental and necessary, take us only so far. Elements of a broader approach to equality of opportunity such as positive action target opportunities to those typically or often excluded from them. Embracing the concepts of diversity and difference further extends your project's commitment to equality of opportunity by requiring you to recognise explicitly the complexities of multiple and often conflicting social identities in the project design and management processes.

Inclusion refers to a strategy which extends the commitment to diversity and difference into all elements of the project. It is much more than 'being comprehensive' or trying to ensure everyone is included in everything you do.

At the centre of an inclusive approach are the concepts of **openness** and **partnership**.

Openness refers to the aim of bringing into the project all those who can be said to be stakeholders in its activities and objectives, and all those who have a genuine interest in its work.

Partnership working involves ensuring that decision making is transparent and gives equal chances to all stakeholders to shape the process and the decisions.

It is perhaps now not difficult to see how this approach can be a vehicle for challenging patterns in the distribution of power between groups, communities and organisations. In any geographical area there will be those who believe that their current influence on what happens in that area is helpful and generally beneficial to the area. Such beliefs may be strongly held and passionately protected. It is worth noting here that an inclusive approach to project design and management, with the emphasis on partnership and openness, may disturb these existing patterns of influence and power.

There are three key operational elements to delivering the first dimension – openness – of an inclusive approach to project design and management:

- Open membership
- Getting engagement
- Maintaining engagement.

Open membership is an ideal and is very difficult to achieve in practice. A fully open membership of the project steering group, for example, may produce an unwieldy and even unworkable group in terms of 'getting the business done' effectively and efficiently. Nevertheless, inclusive practice demands that ways are found to be inclusive without sacrificing completely the effectiveness and efficiency of project decision making. Of course, the

141 ***P01IKRV23*** 21

NEWCASTLE COLLEGE

Routing	***5**
~~Sorting~~	
~~Catalog~~	
Sorting	
Y15D05Y	
Inpro	
Covering — BXAXX	
Despatch	

152337029 ukrwts12 RC1

Ship To: UK 20446033 F
NEWCASTLE COLLEGE
PARSONS LIBRARY
RYE HILL CAMPUS, SCOTSW00
NEWCASTLE
TYNE AND WEAR
NE4 7SA

Volume:
Edition:
Year: 2012
Pagination: 480 p.
Size: 28 x 22 cm

ISBN	Qty	Sales Order
9781444156065	1	F 16081679 1

Customer P/O No   **Cust P/O List**
P100726   25.99 GBP
Title: CACHE level 3 extended diploma for the
children and young people's

Format: P (Paperback)
Author: Smith, Maureen
Publisher: Hodder Education
Fund:
Location: MAIN
Loan Type:
Coutts CN: 18167046

Order Specific Instructions

COUTTS INFORMATION SERVICES LTD.:

quality gains from a diverse membership (i.e. the input of diverse perspectives, experiences and skills) will need to be weighed against potential reduction in efficiency of decision-making. This is, therefore, a balancing act.

One solution is to establish a core membership of the group with sub-groups: the latter with perhaps a more diverse membership than the former which act to drive the agenda and inform the debates of the core group.

Whatever the solution, the key is to ensure that processes for establishing membership of key decision-making bodies are wholly transparent and can be seen to be attempting to ensure appropriate open membership.

Getting engagement is critical to the success of this strategy. It involves, centrally:

■ An open, regular, and clear communications strategy

■ Inclusive opportunities to engage

■ Clear and transparent objectives.

An **open and clear communications strategy** requires

■ A proactive approach to providing information through diverse media

■ Integration into the communications strategy of methods for feedback from all stakeholders and means for the project team to respond to that feedback

■ Regular monitoring of feedback

■ Regular provision of responses to stakeholders about what they have said in their feedback.

Providing **inclusive opportunities to engage** requires as a minimum:

■ Imagination and variation in venues, and times/dates, for meetings

■ Using means other than meetings to maximise engagement – email, a website, post etc

■ Full awareness among everyone working on the project, and among stakeholders, of what the outcome of engaging with the issues is anticipated to be: policy decision, discussion paper, agreement to take responsibilities etc.

However, it is insufficient to provide varied means of engagement without also being clear about what you want people to do, why, and what they can expect as the outcome of all this effort. This latter point emphasises the importance of expressing objectives in ways which will be clear to a diverse audience.

This is as important for specific objectives as for strategic ones. In both cases it is imperative to be clear and to remind everyone, from time to time, of the overall project objective(s). It is all too easy, as a project manager who lives with them daily, to assume that members of task or steering groups (who will likely have other roles/duties/obligations) also carry these with them every day. Equally, it is vital to regularly review the language you are using to communicate your aims and objectives. Again, it is all too easy to become so familiar with the specialist, technical or simply accepted language of your project field that you forget that many stakeholder or interested groups are not immersed in this environment.

What is **partnership** working and how does it relate to 'equality'?

In essence, partnership is about sharing power.

It is simultaneously an exciting and threatening approach. It can be exciting because it opens up possibilities for new ways of working and approaching issues. It is threatening because it can destabilise traditional ways of working and established patterns of individual and/or institutional influence. This is the key to unlocking an inclusive approach to project design and management. Partnership working is dealt with in greater detail in Chapter 5.

At the 'end of the (project) day' an inclusive strategy requires some significant rethinking of power relations – whether between groups, individuals, and/or organisations.

Action checklist

■ List groups, organisations and/or communities which are your focus.

■ Are there any groups or communities, which might have a legitimate interest in, and contribution to make to, your project aims not included in your first list?

■ Am I still excluding anyone with a legitimate interest or contribution to make?

■ Is my communications strategy designed to maximise engagement of all those now considered essential to the success of the project?

■ Are the purposes, membership and ways of working of the committees or decision-making bodies in my project clear and transparent to everyone?

■ Are the project aims and objectives clear and transparent to everyone?

■ Am I clear, and is everyone else clear, about what is expected of them in helping the project achieve its goals?

Summary

Trying to ensure the design and management of your project promotes **equality of opportunity**, embraces **diversity** and **difference**, and is ultimately as **inclusive** as possible is not as difficult as some would suggest, as I hope this chapter has demonstrated.

It does require, however, that you adopt a **reflective management** style and approach. It is no coincidence that throughout this chapter we have emphasised repeatedly the need to be **proactive** and to **consciously** consider certain key issues. It is also no coincidence that the action checklists are constructed most often in terms of questions you will need to ask yourself when designing and managing policies, procedures or activities in order to meet the criteria for good equality of opportunity and inclusive practice.

Asking yourself **honest questions** about your project and your management practices in relation to equality, diversity and inclusivity is fundamental. Doing this regularly is also crucial to success. But all this critical self reflection is pointless if, at the end of the day, you are not prepared to accept that the answers to your honest questions require (maybe some significant and challenging) changes to your project and even to your management of it. The rewards in terms of the ways in which you and your project will be viewed and the impact it is likely to have, are difficult to overestimate.

CHAPTER FIVE

Managing people
and partnerships

In order to deliver the project that has been conceived, developed and planned it is important to ensure that there are adequate resources and capacity available for delivery. The most obvious resource that is needed is the funding or budget allocation – without this very little will be achieved and, as identified in Chapter 2, this is one of the constraints within which a project will operate.

The project will also need to identify physical resources, for example equipment such as PCs or laptop computers and photocopying facilities, or office space where the project manager and team can be based. In planning the delivery of your project the constraint of time also needs to be taken into account as a resource as it can impact on the level of resources and capacity which need to be built into the specification and project plan. Both these aspects of managing resources are discussed in Chapter 6.

However, whilst you may have been very successful in developing a robust specification, gaining approval for funding and drawing up a project plan and schedule, you will need to ensure that your **human resource** is in place. There is no question of doubt that good project management planning techniques and mechanisms for control are essential for success; ultimately it is people who make it all happen.

Adequate human resource is key and is encompassed in a range of sources, both internal to and external to the team of people who are actually delivering the project activity.

This chapter will consider the key relationships that need to be established as part of developing a project, the broad range of individuals and organisations you may encounter and how you can manage these to achieve the greatest impact and success of your activity.

Involving others

As part of effective project management, it is important to remember that the focus is not just on the project delivery team and the beneficiaries. There will be a range of other organisations, bodies and agencies who can make a valuable contribution to the development, delivery and impact of the project, and the size of your project will determine the number of people involved in its development and delivery.

In the planning and development of a project specification, knowledge and expertise will be drawn on from a range of organisations, bodies and agencies. Many of these will have been identified as part of the research phase of the project described in Chapter 1.

These individuals and organisations will become **stakeholders** in the project, some will be **partners** and some will become involved in the governance of the project as a member of the **project steering group**. All will have contact and interaction with the **project manager** and **project team**.

You also need to be aware that there may be other organisations that have not participated in the development phase of the project but who need to be involved. It is essential to draw on the knowledge and expertise of all key organisations in order that project delivery is as inclusive and appropriate as possible. This will enable you to develop an inclusive approach and to begin to challenge the 'deficit model' of 'disadvantaged' groups or communities referred to in Chapter 4. It will also enable you to think in the round about the project, helping to anticipate more effectively where and how delivery may be improved and a greater impact achieved. During the course of planning and delivery you need to review on a regular basis which organisations you are involving and how to go about it.

Although an inclusive approach should be taken to consultation and engagement, you should also bear in mind the need to manage the project partnership. It is easy to lose sight of the organisations whose contributions are most relevant and will have the greatest impact on the success of the project.

Involving others in the project is extremely beneficial. You are able to share the experience of those working in a similar field and it enables you to gain a wider perspective in respect of the need for the activity, what the requirements of the project might be and what you might realistically expect to achieve in your timescale. It also enables you to tap into a wider knowledge base than you might have individually, particularly regarding the needs and expectations of the beneficiaries themselves. This broad involvement, both internally and externally to the project, will not only have a positive impact for the project itself but will also, in many instances, bring benefit to those bodies and organisations you are working with.

Case Study – Creative Learning Project

The Creative Learning Project was initiated by the Arts Council and aimed to re-engage young people who are not in employment, education or training (NEET) back into learning through drama activities. The project also aimed to provide support, information, advice and guidance to help the young people carry on learning after the project had finished.

The project was delivered by outreach workers with backgrounds in creative arts and who had experience of working with a diverse range of young people. The project team recognised that whilst they had the skills and expertise to develop the activities, identify groups of young people and deliver successfully, they needed to interact with other local organisations and agencies who had contact with the NEET group to gain the broadest perspective on the best way to recruit a group of young people and what their particular needs and expectations might be.

The team therefore contacted statutory and voluntary youth organisations and groups who operated in the local area to ensure their involvement with the project. As a result the team were able to gain advice on timing of sessions, location and the type of subject matter that could be tackled. The youth organisations/groups also arranged focus groups of NEET young people to help the project team develop appropriate activities and meet the young people's expectations. Not only was this invaluable for the project team at development stage but they also worked with the focus group to help them evaluate the project.

The project team contacted Connexions, part of whose remit is to provide services to young people in the NEET group. The team wanted to engage with Connexions Personal Advisers who could make contact with the beneficiaries and provide the information, advice and guidance element of the project. By taking this approach the project was ensuring that this element would become sustainable after project delivery was complete. In addition, Connexions benefited from an appropriate mechanism to make contact with a group of young people with which it had previously found it very difficult to work, and enhanced their own practice by gaining a better understanding of their NEET client group.

By making contact with organisations who had an interest in the target group, the *Creative Learning Project* was able not only to enhance the success of its own delivery, but also provide added value to the work of the youth organisations and groups by introducing a new and innovative activity to engage young people which could be delivered by those groups after the lifetime of the project. It also enabled Connexions to become involved in an activity for a group of young people who it had previously not been able to re-engage. A successful outcome all round, and particularly for the NEET target group, will be sustainable beyond its life cycle.

As the example above shows, even for the most innovative of projects there will be other initiatives that are working with the same or similar target groups. By seeking out such initiatives and linking with them you may be able to bring added value and ensure that the project has a greater impact for the beneficiaries involved.

It is worth putting effort into this type of networking early on in the life of the project as it can be a key element in the marketing of and recruitment to the project – see Chapter 3 for more on this.

Stakeholders

The stakeholders in any project are those parties who have an interest in project activities and their delivery. They may be both internal and external to the organisation which has proposed and planned the project and is providing a base for the project team. It is important to recognise that not all stakeholders will be avid supporters of your project activity and that you will need to use your best negotiation, persuasion and communication skills to ensure that they are all engaged.

To help you do this it is worth spending time assessing the project's potential stakeholders to gain an understanding of how they might fit in. Some of the points to be considered could include:

- What is their interest in the project?
- Why are they interested – do they expect to benefit in some way?
- Do they have skills, knowledge or experience to contribute?
- Could project activity adversely affect their own delivery or vice versa? (This could also be regarded as a potential risk to the project – see Chapter 6.)

If your project has many stakeholders it is useful to compile a **stakeholder database** which could include not only names and contact details but also information on whether they are internal or external stakeholders and whether their interest in the project is high or low. The database will prove to be a useful tool in ensuring that good communication and information sharing is maintained.

The funder

The body which has granted the funds has a clear stake in the successful delivery of the project. The funder needs to know that their money is being used appropriately and effectively and is delivering the agreed outputs within budget and on time. The funder will also have a keen interest in the evaluation of the impact of the project activity and outcomes. This will influence how future funding is allocated.

Case Study – Health Care Placement Scheme

A suite of projects has been commissioned by the Learning & Skills Council (LSC) to address skills shortages in the health care sector. It needs to identify cost effective activity which will lead to the take up of education and training to meet the identified skills shortages.

The Health Care Placement Scheme is a pilot project which aims to encourage a greater take up of education and training opportunities in the health care sector by providing thirty work placement opportunities and specific information, advice and guidance to thirty Year 12 students in local further education colleges.

Despite its small budget and ambitious targets the project has succeeded in delivering all its outputs, on time and to budget. Qualitative evaluation also demonstrates that the students who have participated have found both the work placements and IAG very helpful and 95% have progressed onto health care related education and training.

As a result the LSC granted further funding for the roll out of the project to other areas.

As a result of putting an evaluation strategy in place at the outset of the project, the team has been able to demonstrate clearly the positive and cost effective impact it has made, in addition to merely achieving its outputs. You will see from this example how the delivery of project activity not only provides outcomes for the core partners, the FE colleges, but also has a positive impact on other organisations' delivery and outcomes – the LSC in this instance. The project is also able to demonstrate its contribution to a broader regional need in addressing skills shortages in the health care sector.

It is important to keep in touch with the funder through regular updates and reports – it may be that a report is required at the same time that the project team has to complete monitoring forms and/or draws down funds – for example on a quarterly basis. It is useful to build these requirements into either your PERT chart as a scheduled task or Gantt chart as a milestone (see Chapter 2).

Internal stakeholders

Many projects will need to access support services from those who work elsewhere in the organisation providing a home for the project team. These may be related to financial management, professional guidance or human resource services. Usually the identified internal stakeholder will be the line manager of those staff who are required to deliver these support services.

Excellent lines of communication need to be maintained with internal stakeholders as their support and co-operation are vital to the smooth running of the project. It is important to remember that internal stakeholders will have their own agenda, namely that their own department runs effectively and smoothly – they may see involvement in your project as an unwelcome distraction for their own staff.

It is therefore important to gain commitment and 'buy in' at the earliest possible stage. This will mean communicating the project schedule and requirements at project start up stage. In this way constructive negotiations can take place and clear definition be given to activities and the demands on the staff involved.

It is always useful to remind internal stakeholders of the benefit that your project will bring to the organisation as a whole if you find they are somewhat reluctant participants!

Case Study Example – Internal Stakeholders in the 'Health Care Placement Scheme'

The Health Care Placement Scheme is funded by the local LSC and as part of the project monitoring schedule they require quarterly progress reports on activity delivery and financial expenditure. The project team is based in one of the partner FE colleges which is providing all support services through its central functions.

The project manager discovered that when the project proposal was put together no consultation took place with the finance department on their involvement, which is key, given the requirements of the funding stream. The project manager will need the finance department to provide quarterly management accounts in order that accurate financial reports can be submitted to the LSC and to ensure that project spend is being reflected accurately in the accounting system.

The project manager therefore set up a meeting with the departmental director and the line manager of those staff who will be directly involved in providing the required information. The project manager set an agenda in advance of the meeting to ensure that the departmental staff could see that this was to be a process of negotiation rather than a set of demands by the project.

At the meeting the project manager was able to agree to a schedule of dates for the provision of information from the department and clearly outlined the scope of information required. At the same time, the project manager agreed to provide a forecast of spend across the project lifetime so that all information was shared and both teams could have an overview. The staff line manager was invited to sit on the project management group and the departmental director invited to participate in the project steering group.

As a result of this meeting the project manager was able to outline how the involvement of the department would contribute to the success of the project and what the 'knock on' effect for the college might be – further funding, greater opportunities for learners, widening participation and access to the FE provision.

The fact that the Finance Department had not been involved at an earlier stage in the development of this project could have created a significant barrier to the successful delivery to meet funding requirements. However, by setting up the meeting with relevant departmental staff members the project manager demonstrated to the director how the department had a stake in the project, created involvement and started the process of building a good working relationship with and gaining the trust of the department.

External stakeholders

The vast majority of grant or publicly funded projects are outward facing – their purpose is to provide benefit for a particular target group. Such projects will therefore need to ensure that they engage effectively with all relevant external stakeholders. These, for example, could include:

- Organisations and agencies who are already working with the target group

- Statutory agencies working in a related activity field

- Voluntary / community sector groups

- Local employers

- Other private sector organisations.

The stakeholder database is a useful tool in gaining an overview of a project's external stakeholders.

The same principles apply to external stakeholders as to internal. Commitment and 'buy in' are essential in ensuring that external stakeholders do not, either intentionally or unintentionally, place barriers in the path of successful project progress.

Case Study Example – External Stakeholders in the 'Health Care Placement Scheme'

We have already seen how the Health Care Placement Scheme is impacting on the work of its funder and how it is developing relationships with internal stakeholders. It also needs to work with external stakeholders to ensure that any potential obstacles to the successful implementation of the work placement opportunities and the IAG programme are minimised.

The project team knows that participants can be recruited from the

▶

participating FE colleges and that they have agreed to provide the IAG programme through their own specialist Health Care staff. However, the team are also aware that other agencies, particularly Connexions, are providing IAG to this particular cohort. It is therefore important for the project team to ensure that they maintain a good working relationship with Connexions. Connexions might see this project's activity as a threat to their own core activity and consequently communicate a negative view of the project to other stakeholders or partners.

As with the internal stakeholder (the Finance Department) the project manager set up an early meeting with the relevant senior manager in the Connexions service and again set out the purpose and agenda for the meeting in advance.

As part of the meeting the project manager clearly outlined the rationale for the project, its aims, objectives and scope. In this way the project manager demonstrated that the project would not encroach on the work of Connexions as the IAG provided was to be of a specialist nature.

At the same time the project manager suggested that the project could provide added value to Connexions' core services by providing a referral system for young people who do not require the specialist IAG. In addition, the project manager offered to provide IAG resources for Connexions advisers to develop their knowledge of opportunities in the health sector and suggested that Connexions advisers could refer young people with specific health sector IAG needs to the project where they were unable to access the specialist information required.

The project manager also invited the Connexions senior manager to sit on the steering group to ensure continued involvement.

In turn the Connexions manager undertook to inform their front line advisers about the project to ensure they were aware and engaged.

By being able to demonstrate how the project will provide added value to the Connexions service the project manager was able to enhance both the delivery of project activity and the delivery of core Connexions services. The project manager also ensured the continued engagement at senior management level through involvement in the steering group.

Partners

Whilst all project stakeholders will have an interest in the project and have a role to play in ensuring a successful outcome, they are not necessarily partners in a delivery context, although some will be.

Case Study Example – Partners in the 'Health Care Placement Scheme'

If we again consider the Health Care Placement Scheme, it is easy to see that the local NHS Trust where the work placements are to take place is a key stakeholder in the project and this engagement will have been secured at the project development stage at senior management level. However, they will also have a partner role. NHS practitioner staff will have a direct delivery role as they will be supervising students on work placements.

It may well be that NHS senior management have communicated effectively with front line staff who will be working with the students, but they may not have done so. The project team therefore liaised with the relevant NHS senior manager to identify the key delivery staff involved.

It may be that some NHS staff see the work placement activity as a burdensome addition to their everyday workload so it is up to the project team to communicate the aims and objectives of the project with enthusiasm and ensure that the activity is made as straightforward as possible. The project team set up a meeting with all those involved in delivery within the Trust and, as with senior management, clearly communicated the key aspects of the projects in order to secure engagement and 'buy in'.

The roles and responsibilities of project and NHS staff were discussed and agreed at this meeting, as was the process for ensuring that the work placement students were clear about what was required of them on the programme. Any paperwork requirements were discussed and agreed as were reporting and invoicing arrangements (where appropriate).

In order to ensure that effective lines of communication were established and maintained, a member of the project team took responsibility for meeting with the NHS delivery team on a regular

▶

> basis. The NHS delivery team also identified a representative to attend **project management meetings** (see 'The project manager' below).
>
> The project manager took responsibility for keeping the relevant NHS senior management informed of activities and progress in order that they could provide support for their own staff and also ensure that if issues arose support could be provided for the project team to ensure effective delivery.

In this particular project the NHS participated both as stakeholder and partner. The project team had identified mechanisms to ensure that appropriate engagement was secured for both roles. The key to maintaining both levels of relationship is excellent communication, clearly defined roles and responsibilities and a proactive, solution-focused approach from the project manager and team.

This would seem to be straightforward enough. However, particularly in publicly funded activities, we often refer to **partnership working**. This relates to the broad partnership that includes our stakeholders and will be addressed in 'Effective and successful partnerships' below.

Project partners will have an involvement in the delivery of project activity. It is important that the project plan and schedule takes account of the different types of partners it may be working with.

Time constraints and human resource capacity need to be considered in order that partners remain engaged and do not feel that the project is impacting on their ability to delivery their core services. This is particularly relevant if voluntary or community organisations and groups are involved.

The voluntary/community sector is reliant on its volunteer workforce for the delivery of many of its core services. In addition paid staff often work part time. It is therefore essential that consultation takes place with these organisations to ensure that delivery on your project does not become burdensome. It is easy for volunteers to feel 'taken advantage of', become demotivated and disengaged (see 'Implementing the project plan' and 'Working with volunteers' below).

Remember:

- Work up the project schedule in consultation with partners
- Take account of the constraints that some organisations may work within
- Communicate the aims and objectives of the project clearly and with enthusiasm – particularly important when working with volunteers.

The other distinguishing feature of project partners is that they are able to learn and develop directly as a result of their involvement. This experience can be disseminated to the broader stakeholder group for them to draw on in their own organisations.

Implementing the project plan

Information about stakeholders and partners and their roles in the project can and should be incorporated into the project plan. With this in mind, the project now needs to be implemented and delivery commenced. The way in which each individual and partner is involved in project delivery will vary depending on their circumstances and the role they are to play. This section takes a look at some common roles within a project, and also the limitations and constraints that individuals or organisations may face when becoming involved in a project.

The project manager

The project manager's role is to take overall responsibility for ensuring that project outputs are achieved on time and to budget.

In order to do this the manager needs to:

- Plan and organise effectively, using appropriate project management tools (see Chapter 2)
- Oversee and control the delivery of project activity
- Report and disseminate project progress
- Manage the project team and partner input
- Maintain effective and appropriate relationships across project partnerships.

In managing the project team and working to maintain partnership engagement, the project manager must constantly promote the aims and objectives of the project. This will provide a focus and a reminder of why the activity is being undertaken. The project manager must be able to communicate this message effectively and needs to develop a proactive and enthusiastic approach to delivering the project.

Project management tools in the form of PERT and Gantt charts are essential accessories for all project managers (see examples in Chapter 2). They are multi-functional and will assist the manager in the following ways:

i) *Identifying responsibilities for each project team member*

A Gantt chart lends itself well to the inclusion of the assignment of responsibility against a task. The chart provides a visual map of roles and responsibilities within a project team.

ii) *Tracking and demonstrating project progress*

Both Gantt and PERT charts can be used to track progress. This is useful when compiling reports for the steering group, disseminating information to stakeholders, evaluating the project approach and identifying potential sticking points or areas of risk.

iii) *Reviewing and tracking resources*

In the same way as charts can be used to track progress, they can also be used to take an overview of project resources – both team and partner capacity and the time constraint. The manager is able to identify where adjustments need to be made in order that all outputs are met.

iv) *Team motivational tool*

A good project manager ensures that through their own enthusiasm and drive they motivate their project team to perform well. There is nothing better than visually demonstrating what the team has achieved and providing a collective pat on the back. A Gantt chart provides a good visual aid for this purpose as it is drawn up as a timeline and contains project milestones.

In addition to being adept at the application and use of project management tools, project managers need to be good communicators, as mentioned above. Communication is the key to maintaining partnership engagement and effective working relationships. Managers need to ensure that communication with the project team, project partners and stakeholders is:

- Timely – make sure that information is circulated at the right time to be informative and useful

- Appropriate – as useful as email is, sometimes a phone call would be better

- Complete – provide full information, not half a story, and to all those who are relevant

- Consistent – keep in touch with the team, all partners and stakeholders on a regular basis.

The project manager will also drive the management or governance structure. Regular **project management meetings** with the project team and partners are operational and essential for the ongoing management of day-to-day delivery and progress. The project management tools referred to above are a useful focus for these meetings.

The project manager will also have direct input into the **project steering group** (see below).

The project team

The implementation and delivery of the project will revolve around its project team. It will be made up of individuals with a range of skills and expertise related to the needs of the project.

Case Study Example – The Project Team in the 'Creative Learning Project'

The Creative Learning Project is working with the specific target group of young people who are not in employment, education or training, re-engaging the young people through drama activities. The target group comes from diverse backgrounds, including minority ethnic communities and will be recruited largely through local statutory and voluntary youth organisations.

As part of the project's development, the experience, skills and expertise that will be needed to deliver the project effectively were identified, taking into account the target group and its diverse make up. In addition to good project management skills across the team the following were highlighted as essential for successful delivery:

▶

■ Understanding of the voluntary/community sector

■ People, partnership and communication skills

■ The teaching/facilitating of creative arts and drama activities

■ IAG expertise and experience

■ Expertise and experience of working with groups of young people in a challenging environment

■ Language skills for providing information to parents of young people from minority ethnic backgrounds.

The above list informed job descriptions and person specifications. These were considered alongside the activity and outcomes that the project was committed to deliver in order to establish the number and nature (full time/part time) of posts needed.

Understanding the human resource requirements of the project at the outset will facilitate the recruitment of an appropriate team. It will also ensure that the project team contains adequate capacity for efficient and effective delivery.

The role of project team members will include:

■ Undertaking specific tasks which will have specific outcomes and will need to be delivered within an agreed timescale

■ Informing the project manager of progress and updating on issues which may arise

■ Participating in project management meetings

■ Taking responsibility for effective communication with all partners and stakeholders.

Good team morale has a significant impact on the rate and quality of delivery of a project. Team members need to feel valued and that no one member is more important than another. The project manager is responsible for ensuring that all team members are able to perform to the best of their ability and access personal and professional development opportunities. The time-bound nature of project activity and associated fixed-term staff contracts means that all project managers should ensure that their team members have the opportunity to develop and are equipped to move on.

Working with volunteers

Volunteers warrant a special mention as partners in project delivery, as quite often projects which operate in the public sector rely on volunteer involvement to ensure effective delivery. Volunteers are generally motivated in the same way as the project team – all have a commitment to making positive changes for the project beneficiaries. However, they give up their time as a result of personal commitment, unlike salaried project staff who certainly believe in what they are delivering but are doing it to earn a living.

It is therefore important to remember the particular constraints that should be taken account of when engaging a volunteer workforce to help deliver project activity. The following list highlights some of the factors to consider:

- Volunteers are not paid for the work they undertake on behalf of the project. However, they may well be entitled to expenses. This needs to be communicated clearly to all volunteers so they do not feel 'out of pocket' as a result of their involvement. Such expenditure needs to be built into the project budget forecast.

- Some volunteers may be undertaking their voluntary work in addition to paid employment. It is therefore important to be aware of the amount of time that a volunteer can afford the project and when it can be given. Ensure that you make your programme of activities realistic given volunteer time constraints.

- Similarly, always remember that volunteers will have other life commitments, e.g. caring responsibilities. This may also constrain the amount of time they are able to devote to project activity. It could also mean that they may not be able to fulfil their commitment to the project at short notice. Be prepared – always have a back up plan. The project manager and team or other ready resource needs to be able to step in to fill the gap.

- Essential qualifications for undertaking voluntary work are to be committed to and interested in the areas of work the project is undertaking. These may be the only qualifications that volunteers possess. You may find that some of your volunteers have no formal qualifications. It will therefore be particularly important to be aware of their personal development needs. In addition, remember that although not formally qualified, their experience of working with the beneficiary group and their local knowledge are extremely valid and a great resource.

■ Volunteers are often not just motivated because they identify with the project activity and wish to affect change. Many also volunteer for personal development reasons. The project team need to be aware of the development needs of their volunteers and ensure that they have the opportunity to fulfil their own personal goals as part of participating in the delivery of project activity.

Case Study Example – Volunteers in the 'Creative Learning Project'

As part of project delivery the project team for the Creative Learning Project identified that they would be more successful in keeping the NEET target group engaged in project activity by providing them with mentoring support.

The team did not have the capacity, nor did they consider it appropriate for them to deliver this mentoring support themselves. Therefore volunteers working with a partner voluntary youth group were recruited to undertake this role. However, whilst they were very experienced in working with the target group of young people, the volunteers did not have specific mentoring experience.

The project team sourced some appropriate training through their local education authority and established the duration of training and cost. They also found that the training was accredited. The project manager gained authorisation for the project to meet the cost of the training. She also confirmed that the volunteers were prepared to undertake mentoring training, in addition to the work they were already doing for the project.

All arrangements were made for the training by the project team and details communicated in good time to the volunteer team. All volunteers enrolled and completed the accredited course.

By making this training available, the project team ensured that project delivery was more effective and also provided the volunteers with a development opportunity. The project benefits from successful outcomes, beneficiaries gain a quality experience and the volunteers achieve accredited training, building their confidence and making them feel valued.

By its very nature, a team of volunteers will be diverse. The project team should be aware of the different needs of each volunteer but at the same time must keep them all motivated and focused on delivering a successful outcome for the project. This means careful and sensitive management. Excellent communication and organisation are essential for the good management of your volunteer workforce. The following tips will help you take this forward:

- Make sure you communicate the aims, objectives and scope of the project clearly to all volunteers. Ensure they are understood and that volunteers are comfortable in promoting the project on your behalf (if they aren't they are probably not the right volunteers to be working with).

- Draw up a job description, highlighting responsibilities, together with a clear outline of what the volunteers are expected to deliver. In this way the volunteers understand what their role is within the project.

- Arrange regular meetings so that you can keep in touch with volunteers, keep them motivated and receive reports on progress to date and any issues that might have arisen. Always arrange these well in advance so that volunteers can fit the meetings in with their other commitments.

- Always prepare an agenda for meetings and give volunteers the opportunity to contribute to its content. This will ensure that the 'business' of the meeting is achieved. However, an informal approach to management meetings is useful so that volunteers feel confident about contributing their thoughts and ideas.

- Make sure meetings highlight success and find solutions to problems that may have arisen. Don't forget you need to keep your volunteers committed and interested, so be enthusiastic, encouraging and supportive.

- Maintain open lines of communication at all times – be available.

- If your volunteer team have been recruited directly by the project and are not part of a partner organisation, remember that you are their main source of support, providing focus, direction and structure. In this circumstance you can encourage your volunteers to develop a peer support network to provide additional support and motivation.

Relationships with volunteers need to be cultivated and nurtured to build trust. Although it can sometimes be time-consuming it is worthwhile as volunteers can make a significant contribution to the success of project activity. It can also be a fulfilling and rewarding experience for the volunteers who should be able to finish the project with greater confidence and new skills.

The steering group

In contrast to the project management group, the role of the project steering group is a strategic one. The key aspects of this role are:

■ Makes informed strategic decisions

■ Sets project priorities

■ Monitors performance of the project

■ Guides and supports the project manager and project team.

At project start up, the membership of the steering group needs to be agreed. Members will be drawn from key stakeholders who have a significant interest in the project activity (see above). It is essential that those with high interest are involved and engaged in order that these organisations can become advocates for the project and its benefits.

For those projects which are grant or publicly funded, steering group members could include:

■ Organisations representing the target group/beneficiaries of the project

■ Senior management from partner organisations

■ Organisations with a statutory delivery role, e.g., Learning & Skills Councils, local authorities

■ Organisations who are delivering similar or complementary activities

■ Organisations with an overview of relevant policy developments in the relevant context, possibly local, district or even regional, e.g. Regional Development Agency, local authorities

■ Organisations in the private sector that have an interest, e.g. employers.

■ Representatives of the project target group.

It is also important to ensure that the steering group is inclusive and that it provides for appropriate representation of all organisations and groups where the project is likely to have an impact. However, a note of caution – in our efforts to be inclusive we may end up with a steering group which becomes so large it is not able to function effectively. Remember that you need the key organisations and groups represented on the steering group and this can often be achieved by tapping into representative bodies rather than having everyone involved round the table.

At its inaugural meeting the steering group needs to appoint a chairperson and deputy chair. This could be undertaken as a formal process with nominations and a vote. This is advisable if the steering group is large and members have not worked together before. If the group is smaller it is likely that a more informal approach will be adopted, with only one member being nominated.

However the chair and deputy are appointed, it is essential that they are dynamic and visionary and able to lead the steering group for the benefit of the project.

Also at this first meeting terms of reference need to be drawn up and frequency of meetings agreed. The terms of reference should define a clear purpose and the boundaries within which it will operate. The key aspect of the group's role, outlined above, will provide a framework for their development.

It is also very helpful to draw up a schedule of dates for the project, taking into account the agreed frequency of meetings. These can then be built into the project PERT or Gantt charts as tasks or milestones.

The project manager is a key point of contact for the steering group, linking the strategic to the operational. The manager needs to ensure that the steering group remain engaged and are provided with the appropriate information for them to fulfil their role.

The relationship between the project manager and the steering group can be drawn as follows:

Project manager	Steering group
• Reports on progress • Provides financial/budget information • Highlights potential issues and risks • Suggests solutions • Keeps the steering group engaged and focused • Communicates consistently and effectively	• Monitors progress against milestones and targets • Approves expenditure • Takes decisions in respect of project changes and mitigation of risk • Provides a resource of knowledge, expertise and experience to the project manager

The project management tools that the project manager has at their disposal are an invaluable asset in working with the steering group. Of equal importance is communication which will maintain effective working relationships between all those involved and ensure that the project remains focused on its original aims and objectives.

Communication

The need to communicate effectively has been referred to a number of times in the chapter. Why is it so important?

The purpose of communicating effectively includes all the things in the following list:

■ Solve problems

■ Prevent misunderstandings

■ Influence people

■ Create change

■ Act as a conduit for the exchange of information

■ Disseminate information

■ Maintain good morale

■ Celebrate success.

There is also another reason for communicating effectively, which has an impact on the way in which the above list happens and is crucial for the success of projects which are outward facing, and that is **trust**.

If we are working in partnership we need to know that we can trust those we are working with to achieve a common goal for the benefit of our target group. We need to know that our partnership operates in an open and honest way. Clearly, partners and stakeholders will have organisational agendas which will not necessarily align completely with our project mission. However these can be taken account of in an environment where partners are seen as having professional integrity.

In order to build that trust here are some examples of good practice that could be employed and pitfalls that should be avoided in order to communicate effectively and build trust:

Good practice	Pitfalls
• Transparency of process – take an open and inclusive approach • Regular meetings • Report on progress at agreed intervals • Provide accurate, complete and timely information • Deliver what you have said you will and on time. If this is not possible let people know • If something has gone wrong be honest and provide a solution • Draw on the knowledge, expertise and experience that exists across all partners and stakeholders	• Lack of or irregular contact with partners and stakeholders • Project manager and project team unavailable • Inappropriate methods of communication • Exclusive communication rather than inclusive – e.g. incomplete circulation lists • Lack of notice for key meetings or events • Lack of opportunity for partners and stakeholders to input or participate in decision making

Remember:

- Effective communication is the key to project success
- There is no substitute for human contact.

Effective and successful partnerships

The purpose of working in partnership in a project context is to provide for the following:

- Successful/effective delivery
- Appropriate methodology and target groups

- Benefit to partners, stakeholders and beneficiaries
- Maximum impact through the sharing of resources, knowledge, expertise and skill
- An inclusive approach
- Mainstreaming and sustainability beyond the project timeframe.

At project start up stage you can enthusiastically engage with the members of your partnership. They are keen to learn about the project, how it might affect or impact on their own delivery and whether there will be benefits for their organisation's own mission. However, maintaining engagement is more difficult. The environment external to our project activity is subject to change – national, regional and local policy develop quickly and will inform shifts in the focus of our partners. Organisational agendas will change and this will impact on the shape of and the relationships within our partnership. As a result the partnership may be fluid with some members dropping out and others coming on board.

Through the process of change, in order for the partnership to remain successful and effective, there needs to be a consistent approach to its operation. The project manager must make sure that the partnership works in the following way:

i) *Maintaining a strategic overview*

The partnership must have a clear vision and leadership which will drive the vision forward – the project manager and the steering group chair will be instrumental in keeping this on the partnership's agenda.

The progress and impact of the project need to be disseminated on a regular basis and linkages with other initiatives and added value highlighted.

ii) *Focusing on the beneficiaries of the partnership*

Ongoing consultation should be undertaken with the beneficiaries of the project. They are important stakeholders within the partnership and the project will have a greater impact if it understands where delivery could be improved and services adjusted to meet needs.

iii) *Building partner participation*

This is where our effective communication comes in again. Partners will remain engaged and participate in an open and honest environment, where others follow agreed procedures and process, and information sharing is transparent.

iv) *Managing performance*

The partnership needs to have access to up-to-date performance management information and evaluative impact assessment reports. This will enable it to make suggestions and take decisions on key project issues as they arise. Ownership of the project management process by the partnership will maximise engagement.

v) *Learning from experience*

Partnerships need to be able to draw on the experience of activities or aspects of project delivery which have not gone well. This can help to identify future risks and more appropriate approaches. They need to respond to evaluation of the project which may identify things which could provide benefit in partnership organisations.

In the same way when things have gone well it is important to celebrate success. This is a celebration, not only of the role of the project manager, project team and delivery partners, but of the whole partnership itself. An inclusive partnership ensures that everyone has a part to play and the power to effect change is shared by all.

Summary

This chapter has considered how to involve others and how to make effective use of human resource to implement the project plan.

It is important to build and maintain relationships with **stakeholders** and **partners** and create a **project team** which can provide the skills, knowledge, expertise and capacity to deliver successfully.

In managing both people and partnerships it is important to:

- Be open and inclusive – everyone has a part to play

- Ensure engagement – people who believe the project will make a difference and have an impact will drive it forward and make it happen

- Communicate effectively and appropriately – as mentioned above, there's no substitute for human contact.

In the public sector, collaboration and partnership working are watch words for successful projects. Effective partnerships will add value and provide greater impact to project activities.

Further Reading

Working with the Voluntary Sector – National Council for Voluntary Organisations
www.ncvo-vol.org.uk/aboutncvo

CHAPTER SIX

Project resources and project risk

A key feature of a project is that it has a fixed level of resource. Chapter 2 introduced the Project Resource Triangle:

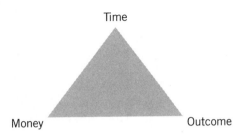

Time

Money   Outcome

The quantity of time and money available to the project is usually fixed at the outset and should be sufficient to deliver the required outputs – in theory! This is where the art of project management comes into play, in balancing the various constraints within a project in order to obtain sufficient resource to deliver the project outcomes within a somewhat unpredictable and changing environment. The money available has to be turned into the resources that are needed to deliver the project, and time has to be used in a way that will achieve the outcomes. Thus, managing resources is at the heart of project management. The efficient use of both time and money is the focus of the first part of this chapter.

The second part of the chapter takes a look at the potential for things going wrong in a project. When working with limited resources and in a set time frame, even small changes can have a major impact on the ability of the project to deliver its outcomes. A proactive approach to risk management can help to overcome the dangers of unplanned change, ensuring that the project is well equipped to be successful despite adverse circumstances.

This chapter only briefly covers one of the major resources involved in a project, people – their time, knowledge and skills. While managing the time of project staff is briefly touched upon here, managing people and partners is covered in greater depth in Chapter 5.

Managing time

Perhaps the most stressful aspect of managing projects is working within a rigid time frame. Most project managers in public, voluntary and community sector organisations have to balance the needs of the project with other projects or responsibilities, so time management skill is an extremely important weapon in the project manager's armoury.

Good time management within a project is very much dependent on how well the project has been planned to start with. A project schedule in the form of a PERT chart, Gantt chart or simply a table provides the raw material for deciding on the best use of time for the project manager and for the whole team. PERT charts are especially useful for highlighting the project's critical path (see Chapter 2) and therefore which tasks it will be essential to finish on time. Gantt charts on the other hand are good for giving a calendar overview of tasks and milestones and can usefully be used as a reference point by the project manager or disseminated to other staff.

Managing your own time

Whichever method is used for project planning, the project manager needs to review the plan on a weekly, or even daily basis, and use it to prepare a 'to-do' list. Making regular to-do lists is a useful discipline. A daily list can be written first thing in the morning or last thing the day before. Items on the list can be prioritised either on a simple 1-3 scale, or by a combination of how urgent they are and how important they are. All tasks can be classified within a 2x2 matrix of urgency and importance, like so:

Urgent, important	Urgent, unimportant
Not urgent, important	Not urgent, unimportant

How tasks are classified depends on the nature of the project and how the task fits in with the overall project plan. Chapter 2 took a look at PERT charts and tasks on the critical path. Anything that affected the critical path of a project would count as both urgent and important. Other tasks not on the critical path may not be so urgent but may still be important. On the other hand, urgent tasks that arise within the organisation that do not directly affect the project, such as having to carry out non-project tasks for management, may be classified as unimportant from a project perspective.

One of the benefits of this kind of classification is that it highlights the tasks that, while not urgent, are still important. Without this kind of methodical approach to time management, these tasks can easily be put off repeatedly or abandoned altogether in the face of the many urgent but fairly trivial tasks that arise from day to day. Focusing on important but non-urgent tasks can make a big difference in terms of the quality of the project, as many planning, monitoring and evaluation tasks come into this category. This is sometimes known as the '80-20 rule' – 80% of the reward comes from 20% of the effort.

It will be clear, therefore, that good planning is an essential component of good time management. When time is short it can be tempting to cut down on planning or bypass it altogether, but without a project plan it is virtually impossible to keep in mind what is truly important to the project, or to keep on track for meeting deadlines. Time spent on planning is never wasted time. It is an investment that will pay back many times over throughout the project's life.

Time management tips

Day to day management of time is all about staying in control rather than allowing external influences to direct your time and attention. The following strategies have been suggested by various time management gurus as ways of maintaining that control and thus freeing up time to work on more important tasks:

■ ***Make some office time.*** Block out some office time rather than filling your diary with wall to wall meetings. You may have to be ruthless about which meetings you miss, or send a colleague along in your place. Sending a junior colleague to attend and report back on a meeting can be a valuable staff development opportunity so there could be a double benefit.

■ ***Make some out-of-office time.*** If you find the office too full of interruptions, work at home on tasks that require concentration. Alternatively, some people find they work well in a café on certain kinds of task. But do ensure that your manager is happy for you to take time out of the office before giving this a try.

■ ***Work with your natural cycle.*** Observe yourself over a period of several days. When are you at your best and sharpest? When do energy levels tend to flag? Some people work much better in the mornings, others don't really get going until the afternoons. Try to work in harmony with your natural pattern by working on creative tasks (such as planning) or scheduling important meetings when you are at your best. Repetitive tasks such as basic administration or filing can be done when you are at your lowest ebb. If your organisation is flexible you might consider changing your work hours so that you start an hour later or earlier.

■ ***Don't wait for phone calls.*** If you phone someone who isn't there, don't get them to call you back. Find out when they are going to be in the office and call them. That way you get to stay in control of your time rather than risk being interrupted when you are busy.

■ ***Cut down interruptions.*** In some job roles it is impossible to cut out interruptions, especially when working very closely with clients or the public. But you may be able to cut down on interruptions at certain times. Having a 'closed door, open door' policy, where people are free to come in if the door is open but not when it is closed, might work as long as the closed door is reserved for times when it is very important not to be interrupted. If you work in an open plan office you may be able to use something else to signal when you shouldn't be interrupted.

■ ***Use travel time productively.*** If you travel a lot, take the train and use the time to catch up on important reading or do some planning.

■ ***Make realistic time estimates.*** When estimating the time that an activity will take, double it to allow time for unplanned interruptions. This is a useful exercise if you frequently find that you have not completed your 'to-do' list by the end of the day.

■ ***Learn how to say 'no'.*** In the public, voluntary and community sectors it can be very difficult to say no to tasks outside your area of responsibility because the culture of the organisation is often one of being helpful. If you find yourself taking on all kinds of additional responsibilities, try this. Instead of automatically saying 'yes', say, 'I'll get back to you on that'. Take a few minutes to think through the request and ask yourself:

 □ How important is this task?

 □ Could anyone else do it?

 □ Could it be achieved in a different way?

 □ Am I inclined to take this on for the wrong reasons?

 □ Do I realistically have time to do this, or will something else important suffer as a result?

Based on the answers to these questions, you may want to negotiate with the person who made the request, and if necessary consult with management. No-one wants to appear unhelpful, but bear in mind that if you are overloaded with tasks then the organisation and its clients will suffer somewhere down the line. If you find it very difficult to negotiate in this way, an assertiveness course might prove helpful.

Managing the time of the project team

It is one thing to manage your own time effectively, but quite another to manage the time of members of the project team, especially as they may not directly report to you within a conventional organisational structure. This is where project management tools really do come into their own. Just as Gantt and PERT charts can be used to prioritise tasks on a personal level they can also be used to prioritise tasks for the whole team. As with everything connected with managing people, communication is key.

One of the stages of project planning was the creation of a work breakdown schedule (WBS) (see Chapter 2). The WBS can be a useful tool in assigning packages of work to individuals or teams of people, or to partner organisations. Because of its hierarchical structure, it is perhaps easier to see how far a project task needs to be broken down into sub-tasks before being handed over than, say, a Gantt chart.

The case study used in Chapter 2 introduced the Skills Audit Project and its work breakdown schedule. In the example on page 29, the area of Audits was broken down into sub-tasks. However, there were three other main branches to the tree – Recruitment, Research and Evaluate:

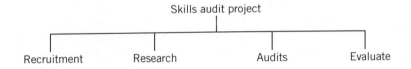

Rather than breaking down the Evaluate area into tasks and sub-tasks, this whole area could have been assigned to a project partner who would be responsible for breaking it down into tasks and scheduling them. Assigning the work can be done as formally or informally as appropriate to the project, but as a minimum it is recommended that the following be agreed in writing:

- Completion date (and start date where relevant) of the work to be completed

- Outcomes to be delivered, with dates

- Milestones to be achieved, with dates (although the partner or staff member may develop these themselves, in which case they should inform you of the milestones so that they can be entered into the project schedule)

- Reporting requirements, including paperwork that has to be filled in
- Budget available for the work.

A formal way of doing this is through a Work Package Agreement Form.

Work Package Agreement Form

Project name	
Work package name	
Named person responsible*	
Description of work	
Start and finish dates	
Outcomes	
Milestones	
Budget	
Signed	
Signature of project manager	

* Even if the work package is being assigned to another organisation it is good practice to have a named person who will take responsibility for the work

Individual tasks can be assigned in a similar way, either to internal staff members or partner organisations. If the project schedule has already been drawn up, information about the dependencies of the task or tasks assigned can also be included. It is a good idea to provide a copy of the overall schedule either in the form of a Gantt or PERT chart when assigning a work package, as this will highlight how the work fits in with other tasks in the project and how any delays or changes might have an impact on other people's work.

Of course rather than simply handing over a form and a copy of the schedule it is essential to talk through the work, discuss any difficulties and allow the staff member or partner to ask questions. This may result in changes being made to the nature of the tasks, the timescales or the budget, which in turn will mean that the whole project schedule will need updating. However, it is better to make changes at an early stage than to face changes when the project is underway.

A Work Package Agreement Form or similar provides the basis for ensuring that others keep to schedule with their part of the project. This allows the project manager to keep track of what outcomes and milestones should be delivered and by when, and provides a level of accountability. The project manager therefore has sufficient information and authority to monitor the different parts of the project effectively. Monitoring will be covered in more detail in Chapter 9.

More in-depth discussion about managing people, and about people and partners as a resource, can be found in Chapter 5.

Procurement of resources

The remainder of this chapter will follow the case study example of 'The Learning Room' project.

Case Study – The Learning Room Project

The Learning Room was set up by a medium sized food processing company, Fidelta Ltd, in partnership with a trade union and a local Further Education College. The purpose of the project was to allow employees to update their work skills and/or to learn for personal reasons. The Learning Room was fitted with a network of fifteen computers which gave access to a wide range of learning materials. The room could also be used as a training centre for up to twenty people.

Procurement is the process of specifying and purchasing goods and services. In other words it is about deciding what you need to spend your project budget on, and then getting the best and most appropriate value and quality possible.

As with most aspects of project management, procurement is linked very closely to project planning. As the project schedule is drawn together, it should be possible to identify where goods and services will need to be bought in. This in turn informs the drawing up of the project budget (see Chapter 7). The stage at which to start thinking about procurement is when the methodology for carrying out the project has been decided, as this will have an influence on what needs to be purchased.

Key questions to consider at this stage are:

- What do we need access to in order to achieve the outcomes of this project using the agreed methodology, in terms of:
    1. Buildings, accommodation or space requirements
    2. Equipment
    3. Consumables (small, consumable items)
    4. Specialist skills and services?

- Which of these resources are: already available; able to be purchased internally; need to be purchased externally?

Case Study Example – Procurement Planning

The following table was initially drawn up for The Learning Room project:

Category	Details	Availability
Buildings etc	Room to accommodate 15 computers, with space to train 20 people in 'theatre style' setup	Fidelta Ltd will provide a suitable room
Equipment	15 computers – require them to be networked and internet enabled	Purchase externally
	1 server	Use of company server
	2 printers	Purchase externally
	1 ceiling-mounted data projector	‘
	1 projection screen	‘
	Desking for 15 computers	‘
	17 computer chairs	‘
	23 folding chairs	‘
	1 large table	‘
	1 small table	‘
	1 photocopier	Lease?
	1 coffee machine	Purchase externally
	2 flip charts	

▶

Category	Details	Availability
Consumables	Printer/photocopier paper Computer disks Coffee Plastic cups Flip chart paper and pens Printer toner Photocopier toner	Purchase
Skills & services	Setup and networking of computers Specialist trainers Evaluation	Fidelta will provide a staff member to do this External contracts External contract

This exercise allowed the project manager to draw up a list of items and services that had to be procured.

Procurement in the UK is governed by fairly strict laws from the EC, especially for public sector companies, which require large purchases to be put out to commercial tender. In addition to this, larger organisations are likely to have existing agreements with suppliers, especially equipment suppliers, which effectively stop staff members from being able to 'shop around'. If working for a public sector organisation, or indeed any larger organisation, it is always advisable to consult with a member of staff responsible for purchasing to ensure that purchases (including contracts for services) meet these regulations.

For larger purchases, even if it is not a legal requirement for the purchase to be put out to tender it may still be useful to go through some kind of tendering exercise in order to ensure the best value for money. Alternatively you may wish to invite expressions of interest or obtain several quotes. The basis for any such decision is to draw up a specification of exactly what you want to buy, and to agree on how much money you are prepared to spend.

Case Study Example – Specifying Services

The Learning Room's steering group wanted to commission a detailed evaluation of the project to examine how effective it was at improving skill levels and motivation among Fidelta's staff. They were prepared to spend up to £22,000 on an evaluation.

A sub-group was formed to draw up a detailed specification of the aims, objectives and scope of the evaluation they required. They then invited several consultancy firms in the region to submit a costed proposal for carrying out the evaluation. At a later meeting of the steering group, the proposals were compared and discussed, and a company was chosen to carry out the evaluation that on the basis of their proposal represented the best value for money.

Other procurement considerations

As well as wanting to obtain the best value for money, other considerations may influence your purchasing and procurement decisions. Organisational policy and procurement law have already been mentioned. Other influencing factors may include:

Ethical purchasing: An ethical stance on purchasing either by the organisation or by the project itself may direct the choice of supply companies. In faith-based organisations this may be linked to tenets and practices of faith. For other organisations or individuals, issues of fair trade or ethical manufacturing policy may be important. As well as the intrinsic benefits of making ethical purchasing decisions there may also be issues of organisational credibility to consider. For example an organisation dedicated to the welfare of children might be badly compromised by making major purchases from a company that used child labour. Ethical purchasing will require a great deal of research into the policies and practices of potential supply companies and some effort may be needed to ensure that there are sufficient ethical suppliers available so that prices can be adequately compared and that value for money is obtained.

Sustainable/Green purchasing: A major ethical consideration when making purchasing decisions may be sustainability. Indeed, a number of funding programmes require that sustainability is addressed within each project they fund. Sustainable purchasing may mean buying recycled or reconditioned products where possible. It may also encompass how resources are managed at the end of their useful life – for example, computer equipment being reconditioned and resold or donated. Another aspect of sustainable purchasing is sourcing products from local suppliers to cut down on the transport costs and the pollution and carbon emissions this causes. Again, sustainable purchasing may be an organisational decision or it may be something specific to the project.

Thought may also be given to the long-term usefulness of project purchases, especially in small organisations that are very reliant on grant funding. A large purchase of craft equipment and supplies, to give an example, may be used for several different projects, which could affect the strategic planning of future projects in order to make best use of this investment.

In short, it is the role of the project manager to use the limited project budget to obtain the equipment and supplies required to deliver the project successfully. This will usually mean balancing between the requirements of quality and value for money, and other considerations may also come into play. Strategic purchasing of equipment may also have significant benefits for future projects within the organisation, or even within partner organisations.

Managing risk

Change is inevitable in a project and managing change is an essential element of the art of project management. Dealing with general changes to the project is covered in Chapter 9. This section looks at dealing with unpleasant and unwelcome changes that may occur during the life of a project – in other words managing risk.

Risk can be defined as the probability of an unpleasant or harmful event happening. Risk management therefore is the process of assessing risk and developing strategies to deal with it. An 'unpleasant or harmful event' in the context of a project could be something that is harmful in some way to:

- The project budget
- The achievement of the project outcomes
- The project timeline
- Project's staff or staff in partner organisations
- Those who benefit from the project

- Any other person directly or indirectly affected by the work of the project

- The project's host organisation

- One of the project partners.

Harm could be defined in terms of failure, physical injury, negative impact on reputation, financial loss or loss of assets.

Risk is not necessarily a negative thing. Any innovative, ground-breaking project is at least a little bit risky, so to try and avoid risk altogether is not the only way to go. Aside from this, there is no such thing as a risk-free project. Every project – indeed every activity – does carry some level of risk even if it is quite small. It is worth remembering this, as some organisations are quite averse to risk, and management may be unwilling to commit to any project that they see as being at all risky.

The good news is that risk avoidance is not the only way to manage risk. In fact risk management is all about shedding light on areas of potential risk and bringing them out into the open so that they can be dealt with. Good risk management practice means that even risky projects can sometimes go ahead because the level of risk is under control. It is uncontrolled risk that poses a problem.

The first step towards managing risk in a project is to identify all the different possible risk areas. At first this can seem like a daunting task, especially if the project is a large one. There are two approaches to this:

- Identify different sources of risk and then identify the risks to the project from these sources

- Look at the project on a task-by-task basis and identify risks attached to each task

The method you choose will largely depend on the type and size of project, although if you are new to risk management you might want to try both approaches to see if you come up with the same results.

Sources of risk

Risks to a project can come from many different areas. For example:

- **Finances**
  Could funding be withdrawn or reduced? What if the project failed an audit? Might a staff member or partner misuse project funds?

- **Staff**

  What if a staff member left or was absent for a long period? What if the project was not able to recruit key staff members? Could a staff member damage the project by acting improperly – for example, offending an important partner organisation?

- **Safety**

  Is there any risk of harm to staff, partners or beneficiaries of the project?

- **Partners**

  What would happen if a key partner withdrew from the project? What if a partner did not carry out their part of the project to the required standards? What if a partner missed project deadlines?

- **Legal**

  Which laws affect the project – Data Protection Act? Procurement law? Disability Discrimination Act? Does the project comply with the relevant legislation?

- **Supplies**

  What if a supplier of goods or services failed to supply on time?

- **Information security**

  What if project data was lost? Does the project hold sensitive information that could be misused or stolen?

- **Resources**

  Could any of the project's physical assets or resources be lost, stolen or damaged?

- **Competition**

  Are there other similar projects in the same area or targeting the same people that might have an impact on your project? Will your project be competing for resources (for example staff time) with other projects or activities?

The above is by no means an exhaustive list, but it does illustrate the breadth of risks that might affect a project.

Once the risk areas have been identified, these will need to be turned into specific statements that relate to the project. The risky events described in these statements are often referred to simply as **events**.

Case Study Example – Identifying Risks

The Learning Room identified risks in all of the categories listed above. Below is an extract from their risk assessment.

Risk Area	Event
Resources	Computer equipment is stolen
	Computer equipment is damaged or malfunctions, taking more than 1 week to repair
	Computer equipment is damaged or malfunctions, taking less than 1 week to repair
Staff	Failure to appoint a suitably qualified and experienced project manager
	Project manager unavailable for more than 2 weeks
	Failure to secure appropriate trainers
	IT Manager (Fidelta Ltd) unavailable for more than 1 week because of sickness or commitment to other work within the company

In the example, the risk statements are phrased as if the event is currently taking place. This is the usual way that risks are described as it makes things clear and avoids complicated phrasing.

When identifying project risks in this way it can be difficult to know where to draw the line. After all there are many, many things that might happen, however unlikely. The list of risks can seem disproportionately large compared to the size of the project and you might wonder if you are being a bit too thorough. What to include is a question of judgement. One way of solving this dilemma is to involve a number of different people in developing the list of risks. These could include team members or project partners. Larger organisations should have a staff member who is experienced in risk management and who might also be able to lend support. The important thing is to bear in mind the following questions when considering a potential risk:

- Is this risk directly related to the activities of the project?
- Is there a realistic chance that it could happen?
- Would it have a genuine impact on the project if it took place?

If the answer to all three is yes then it is better to play safe and list it.

Identifying risk based on individual project tasks or groups of tasks can be appropriate if there are areas of the project that are seen as more risky than others, or where the risks are quite different. This might be the case if, for example, the project included a workshop aimed at young people. In this case issues of health and safety and of child protection might pose risks to the project, but only in relation to the group of tasks relating to the workshop.

Calculating level of risk

Identifying risks to a project usually results in a long list of risks which may seem daunting but not very useful. However, not all risks are equal. The level of risk depends on two things:

- How likely it is that the event will take place?
- What would be the impact on the project if the event took place?

Each of these can be given a numerical value. A common way to do this is by giving a number from 1 to 3 to each of these, where 1=low; 2=medium; 3=high. The two are then multiplied together.

Level of risk = probability of event x impact of event

Using a scale of 1 to 3 gives a result of 1, 2, 3, 4, 6 or 9 for each event to show how high the level of risk is. These can be left as numbers, or can be translated into Low, Medium and High. Sometimes these are represented by traffic light colours – Red for high, Amber for medium and Green for low.

Case Study Example – Calculating Risk

The Learning Room steering group calculated the risk levels for all the risks identified in their risk assessment table. Below is an extract:

Event	Probability	Impact	Risk Level
Failure to appoint a suitably qualified and experienced project manager	1	3	3 – LOW
Failure to secure appropriate trainers	2	2	4 – MEDIUM
IT Manager unavailable for more than 1 week	3	3	9 – HIGH

A member of staff from Fidelta Ltd was responsible for assessing the risk levels. She was aware that a suitably qualified staff member from the college had already expressed an interest in the project manager post, and so was able to assess the probability of the first event as low. On the other hand, she knew that the IT Manager working for Fidelta Ltd, who was to support the IT equipment for The Learning Room, was frequently overworked. Moreover, she knew that he would have to prioritise the commercial needs of the company above the needs of The Learning Room project. She therefore assessed that the probability of him being unavailable to The Learning Room for more than 1 week to be high. This could potentially result in the computers being out of action for more than a week at a time, which would have a serious impact on the project.

The purpose of calculating the level of risk is in order to prioritise, so that the project team can focus on the highest risk events. Without a systematic approach to risk management it is easy to become sidetracked by lower risk events while failing to address much higher risk aspects of the project.

How risks are then managed might depend on the project's lead or partner organisations and it is always worth the project manager consulting with their own line manager when drawing up a strategy to tackle risk.

Risks may be dealt with in four main ways:

- Avoid
- Assign
- Minimise
- Mitigate.

Avoid

Some events may be considered so risky that the project has to be redesigned to eliminate them. For example, a project lead organisation might decide that they are unable to take a group of young people rock-climbing because the risks are unacceptably high. However, we have already said that avoidance is not the only way to manage risk, and there are other alternatives that could be considered first.

Assign

Assigning risk means making it someone else's responsibility to deal with the consequences if the event does take place. This is the basis of insurance. When you insure the contents of your home you are handing over to the insurance company the responsibility of paying for any losses that might occur if your home is burgled. Project risks can be assigned to partner organisations, who will take responsibility for risks attached to their tasks within the project. If this is the case, these responsibilities should be made very clear within any agreement or memorandum drawn up with the partner organisation. This is sometimes done in relation to financial risk. A project partner who is given part of the project budget takes on responsibility for the proper use of that budget and accepts any consequences that might arise from that – for example they may be responsible for repaying funders in the case of an audit failure. By identifying all the project risks in advance, partners can share the risks appropriately and in a way that is clear and transparent to all.

Minimise

For events that register as high or medium risk, steps can often be taken to reduce this level of risk and bring it back down to acceptable levels by decreasing the chance of the event happening. You may have home insurance, but you probably would still lock your door and you might install a burglar alarm to decrease the chances of being burgled in the first place. This can be a good alternative to avoiding risks altogether. Minimising risks might involve setting up new policies and procedures, ensuring staff are properly trained, creating a safe working environment and so on. It is about carrying out project tasks in a less risky manner, even though the tasks may remain the same.

Mitigate

Finally, risks can be mitigated. This means that if the event should take place, something can be done to decrease its impact. Most undesirable events can be mitigated to some degree. For example, if the project manager was to leave, other staff could temporarily take over his or her duties which would minimise disruption to the project. However, mitigation is also about being prepared in advance and having back-up plans. A project manager might decide to train up another member of the project team on project management techniques and allow them to work-shadow the project manager from time to time so that if the project manager did leave then the member of staff could take over project management duties quite effectively until a new manager was appointed. Where high risks cannot be minimised, they can be adequately mitigated by having good back-up plans and preparing for alternative courses of action.

Both minimisation and mitigation decrease the overall level of risk. Going back to our risk equation:

Level of risk = probability of event x impact of event

Minimisation decreases the probability of the event, and mitigation decreases the impact – which is why they will both decrease the overall level of risk. Very high risks can be both minimised and mitigated which will further bring down the level of risk.

The case study below shows how these different approaches to risk can be incorporated into a risk management strategy for the project. This could also be done at the programme level if managing several projects.

Case Study Example – Developing a Project Risk Management Strategy

The steering group for The Learning Room were presented with a summary table of risks to the project, with the highest risks listed first, followed by the medium and then the low risk events. The group discussed their approach to managing the high risk areas, incorporating a mixture of assigning, minimising and mitigating.

Event	Risk Level	Action
Failure to appoint a suitably qualified and experienced project manager	3 – LOW	No action
Failure to secure appropriate trainers	4 – MEDIUM	Minimise by liaising with FE College and with local private and voluntary sector training organisations to identify suitable trainers
IT Manager unavailable for more than 1 week	9 – HIGH	Mitigate by engaging a small IT consultancy firm to provide back-up when IT Manager not available

▶

> The steering group had previously discussed a proposal to open The Learning Room to the general public in the evenings. While some of the risks attached to this, such as public liability and theft of property, could be assigned through appropriate insurance, there remained a risk of threat to staff. This was judged to be high, as a number of shopkeepers in the area had been attacked during evening openings in recent months. The steering group therefore felt that this risk was sufficiently serious to warrant avoiding it altogether, and the plans for evening opening were put on hold for the time being.

Summary

An important feature of the role of a project manager is managing the resources needed to deliver the project successfully.

Time is a key resource and needs to be managed wisely in order to keep to the project schedule. Strategies for managing time can be adopted by the project manager in order to maintain focus on the most important and critical tasks for the project. The time of other project team members and partners can be monitored using scheduling information and tools such as the **Work Package Agreement Form**.

Purchasing the physical, consumable and specialist resources the project needs to succeed is a question of **good procurement practice**. A number of issues may have an impact on how resources are procured, including legislation, organisational policy and, in some cases, ethical considerations. Within these constraints, the project manager's role is to obtain the appropriate quality and the best value for money. Good strategic planning can ensure that, where possible, resources have a use beyond the life of the project.

Risk management is a way of dealing with the unpredictable world in which projects must be delivered. A systematic approach to risk management means identifying, quantifying and dealing with risks before they arise. Risks may be avoided, assigned, minimised or mitigated. Good risk management does not mean the complete avoidance of risk, but rather having the information to proceed with a known level of risk and knowing what to do if the event does occur.

Further reading

Time Management

David Allen – *Getting Things Done: The Art of Stress Free Productivity*. Piatkus Books. ISBN: 0749922648

Procurement

A guide to Construction Project Management in the Voluntary Sector has been published by Sport England and can be found at: www.sportengland.org/management-vol.pdf

The Charities Statement of Recommended Practice (SORP) published in 2005 contains some recommendations about expenditure and resources, with special reference to how they should appear in the charity's accounts, and can be found at: www.charity-commission.gov.uk

Risk Management

Donald Teale – *Project Risk Assessment in a Week*. Hodder Arnold. ISBN: 034084972X

A Voluntary Matters risk management resource: www.voluntarymatters3.org

CHAPTER SEVEN

Project financial management

One of the major constraints on a project is its budget. The amount of funding available to the project is at the root of all decisions about staffing, purchasing supplies and equipment, and ultimately the services that can be offered to project beneficiaries. This chapter looks at issues of costing and managing the project budget, with particular reference to revenue projects. While much of the information presented is also relevant to capital projects, costing building projects is a specialism in its own right and is not covered in detail here, though pointers to further information are given.

As well as looking at how to go about costing a project, the chapter also deals with issues connected with the mechanics of grant-funding schemes, such as match funding and eligible and ineligible costs.

The chapter uses two different case studies to highlight and explore important funding issues and to contrast different costing methodologies.

Case Study One – Make it Happen

The purpose of The 'Make it Happen' project is to work with young people age 16 – 25 who are not in education, employment or training, to help them find a positive direction for their lives. The project is based at a youth centre in a small market town.

The project draws its funding from the Peterson Trust, a local grant-making charitable trust.

Case Study Two – Revive

Revive also aims to help young people in the 16 – 25 age group. Based at an FE College it offers a tailored programme of vocational training, guidance and confidence building for young unemployed people.

The project draws 45% of its funding from the European Social Fund (ESF), 40% from a Lottery funding source and the remaining 15% from the college's own resources.

Estimating project costs

It can be difficult to know where to start when attempting to turn a rough project idea into a fully fledged project budget, especially if you are new to managing projects. There is no one best way to cost a project, as the method used will depend very much on the type of project being proposed and, to an extent, on the type of funding that is being sought. A good place to start is with staff costs. There are (at least!) two basic approaches to estimating **staff costs** for a project:

■ Estimates based on the project schedule

■ Using staff appointments as a basis for costing.

Managers will often use a combination of the two approaches to arrive at a set of costings. If this seems intimidating it is important to remember two things:

■ Project costing is best done as a team effort

■ It is a good idea to work out a rough estimate first and then refine it.

Basing the staff costs budget on staff appointments

This method is often used in the voluntary and community sectors and also in schools, though it may be used in other sectors and contexts too. Using a staff appointments approach to budgeting can be useful where an infrastructure already exists and is paid for and the proposed project wants to build on this. Grant-making trusts will often fund projects on this basis.

Some projects will naturally lend themselves to the creation of one or more job roles. Projects that involve a lot of work of the same type would typically fall into this category, for example:

■ Youth or community work projects

■ Counselling or mentoring projects

■ Teaching projects

■ Outreach work.

How much funding is required will, of course, depend on the level of the appointment and also on the proportion of a post that is to be funded. Other questions to ask include:

■ What will be the level of responsibility of this person, and is this sufficient to achieve the project's aims and objectives?

■ Can one person realistically be expected to have all the skills required by the project or do they need to be supported by others?

■ Will this person take responsibility for project management and monitoring activities, and if so has enough time been built in for this?

■ Who will manage this post and how much time will that take?

If your organisation has a structured grading system this may dictate the costs attached to the proposed post. In some cases it may be important to ensure that the salary of the post is roughly on a level with similar posts in other organisations. This is especially important if the post is not a typical one for your organisation. For example, an outreach worker in a university may be graded on an administration or lecturer grade. In this case it would be important to ensure that pay and conditions of service were at least as good as those offered by other organisations, for example the voluntary sector, otherwise it could be difficult to appoint a suitable candidate. This may require close liaison with Human Resources staff if your organisation has an HR department.

Another consideration is whether this will be a new post, a secondment from your own or a partner organisation, or the continuation of the contract of an existing member of staff. There may be excellent reasons for extending the contract of an existing staff member, especially if their current contract is about to come to an end. They are likely to have the experience required and perhaps will have been involved in the development of the project. However it may be useful to consider whether they have any training needs in relation to the new post, and whether this can be funded by the project.

As well as the salary of the staff member, the organisation will almost certainly be paying some level of on-costs which may include employers' National Insurance and employers' pension contribution. This should be factored into any budget estimates made about staff appointments. Another point to remember is that salaries are likely to go up at least once a year to take account of cost of living increases. In some types of organisations, staff will automatically go up a point on the salary scale each year as well. These need to be taken into consideration, especially if the project is longer than one year.

Case Study Example – Staff Cost Estimates for 'Make It Happen'

Make It Happen was planned to run over a two year period. Because the infrastructure of the youth club was already in place, the main cost to the project was the appointment of a Youth Development Worker to run the project. The estimate of staff cost was calculated as follows:

Youth Worker level 2 scale point 11 (estimate of level on which appointment will be made): £19,629

+

On costs of 18% = (19,629 x 0.18) = £3,533

=

£23,162

It was estimated that a 0.5 (half time) contract would be required in order to carry out the project, so the costs for Year 1 of the project were:

£23,162 x 0.5 = £11,581

For the second year of the project, 6% was added to cover pay rises and promotion. The estimate of costs for the project therefore looked like this:

	Year 1	Year 2	Total
Youth Worker	£11,581	£12,276	£23,857

It was agreed that the project should also budget for some management time to cover the time taken to line manage the Youth Worker and to carry out other tasks related to the project such as attending meetings and project monitoring. About twenty management days per year were estimated for this.

Basing the staff costs budget on the project schedule

The other approach to staff costs is to use the project schedule. This can be a useful way of approaching costing if the project is likely to involve a lot of different people, or if it is a new kind of project to the organisation.

In this case, estimates will be made using the 'duration' information created in the project schedule (see Chapter 2). The number of days' effort can be added up for each different area of expertise to see how much time of different staff members is likely to be taken up by the project.

Case Study Example – Staff Cost Estimates for 'Revive'

The Revive project was designed to run over a one year period. A member of college staff had already created a project schedule. She was then able to use this information to estimate the amount of staff effort, in days, that was likely to be needed:

Task	IT trainer	Soft skills trainer	Other trainers (total)	Guidance staff	Project management and admin
Recruit beneficiaries	0	0	0	0	15
Initial guidance (30 beneficiaries)	0	0	0	15	10
Ongoing learning reviews	3	3	3	30	15
Confidence building		10		2	5
Vocational training	20	5	20	0	10
Work tasters	0	0	0	3	20
Attending meetings	3	3	6	3	20
Planning etc	0	0	0	0	25
TOTAL	**26**	**21**	**29**	**53**	**120**

The project was going to buy out the time of training staff from the college to deliver training sessions. Trainers had been costed as follows:

Average salary of training staff = £21,650 per annum + 16% on-costs = £25,114

Number of days worked per year = 225

Therefore cost per day = £25,114 / 225 = £111.62

So 26 days of trainer time would cost:

£111.62 x 26 = £2902.12

And so on.

Using the same process for all staff, the staff costs were calculated as follows:

IT trainers 26 days @ £111.62 per day	£2,909.12
Soft skills trainers 21 days @ £111.62 per day	£2,344.02
Other trainers 29 days @ £111.62 per day	£3,236.98
Guidance staff 53 days @ £94.37 per day	£5,001.61

Because so much project management and administration time was required, it was agreed to appoint a full time project manager and part time administrator who would be shared between the Revive project and another similar project.

In both the case study examples, each of the two approaches to staff costing was used in the end even though the two project teams approached the task differently.

Other project costs

In addition to staff costs, other costs to the project may include:

- Support to project beneficiaries such as travel expenses or childcare
- Office costs such as rent, utilities etc
- Stationery and consumables
- Small items of equipment
- Large items of equipment
- Building or redevelopment costs.

Some of these will be straightforward to estimate. For example, if a project has thirty beneficiaries who are returners to the labour market, it might be reasonable to assume that twenty of them will need childcare support. If childcare costs approximately £70 per week and the project lasts six weeks then the estimate for childcare costs will be:

20 x £70 x 6 = £8,400

Estimates of capital costs such as building or refurbishment would usually be supplied by builders.

There will usually be some costs that cannot be estimated directly, related to the premises at which the project will be run. For example, it would be reasonable to ask for some contribution towards rent, rates and utilities given that the project team will be taking up space and using resources within a building. The way this is calculated will depend on the requirements of the funders. Some funders will be happy with a reasonable estimate – either a notional figure or a percentage.

Case Study Example – Overhead Costs for 'Make it Happen'

The team initially estimated their costs for using the Youth Centre premises as £2,000 per year. The Peterson Trust supplied guidelines that estimates of premises costs should be approximately 20% of staff costs. This meant that in Year 1 of the project, costs look like this:

Staff costs

Youth worker   £11,581

Management costs   £3,589

Total staff costs   £15,170

Overhead at 20% of staff costs

$$£15,170 \times 20\% = £3,034$$

Using the suggested formula of 20% of staff costs, the Make it Happen project received over £1,000 more than their initial rough estimate. This is significant because it illustrates how often in practice overhead costs are underestimated. As well as costs relating to rent, rates and utilities, a building also requires maintenance and cleaning. There may be staff members such as a receptionist or an accountant who work across all the projects and activities taking place within that building. There may be leased equipment such as a photocopier. All these things cost money and in theory the costs should be shared between projects.

A more formal way of estimating overhead costs, and one that is preferred (or even required) by some funders, is to use an **apportionment methodology.**

The basis of apportionment is to find some variable that is common to all projects or activities – for example, staff time – and divide out all overhead costs by this variable. A simple example will illustrate this.

An organisation has two projects, A and B. There is one member of staff working for the organisation who works 200 days a year, spending 50 days a year on project A and 150 on project B. The rent, rates and utilities costs for the organisation add up to £22,000 per year.

The overhead cost **per staff day** to the organisation can be calculated by dividing the overhead cost by the number of days worked in the organisation per year.

£22,000 / 200 = £110

(This means that for every day the staff member works, it costs £110 in overheads to keep the organisation ticking over.)

Overhead costs for projects can therefore by calculated by multiplying the number of staff days on the project by the overhead cost per staff day.

For project A:

50 staff days x £110 = £5,500

For project B:

150 staff days x £110 = £16,500

You will notice that the overhead costs for projects A and B add up to £22,000. This is as it should be because the two projects are the only two activities taking place within the organisation, therefore between them they need to cover all of the overhead costs otherwise the organisation will be running at a loss.

This example illustrates the basic principles involved, but of course real life is much more complex. The following case study highlights some of the real issues involved in carrying out an overhead apportionment.

Case Study Example – Overhead Costs for 'Revive'

Because the project was based in a fairly large and complex organisation, an overhead apportionment methodology had to be used to estimate the overhead costs of the project. The team met with the management accountants to discuss the best method to use, and they agreed to apportion by student learning hours delivered, as this method had been used in the past.

At the bidding stage, estimates were used based on the previous year's data. When it came to claiming the money from the funders, the figures had to be reworked using current data.

The college had excellent data on the number of student learning hours delivered per year. This worked out at 1,400,000. This was not a figure based on the number of hours that staff taught (teaching hours), but on the number of hours of teaching received across all the students in the college (learning hours). This worked out at 1,600 full time equivalent students having approximately 25 hours teaching and other guided learning activities per week for 35 weeks per year.

Student learning hours was used in preference to teaching hours because the number of students in a class varied so much that using teaching hours did not yield reliable figures.

The overhead costs of the college had to be drawn from the audited accounts. An initial problem with this was that while the project was run over one calendar year, the college's finances were presented based on an academic year. This meant that two sets of accounts had to be used to draw up a set of costs for a calendar year.

To carry out an initial estimate, the team used figures from the previous calendar year, 2004. They drew out the relevant costs, using 7/12ths of the costs from the 2003-4 audited accounts (for the year ending July 2004) and 5/12ths of costs from the management accounts for 2004-5 (as at the time the audited accounts had not yet been prepared).

This resulted in the following table:

▶

Cost category	2003-4 ($^7/_{12}$ of cost)	2004-5 ($^5/_{12}$ of cost)	Total
Rents and rates	£110,000	£84,000	£194,000
Utilities	£357,000	£269,000	£626,000
Telephones	£176,000	£127,000	£303,000
Books and learning materials	£56,000	£37,000	£93,000
Stationery and postage	£47,000	£35,000	£82,000
Lease rentals	£18,000	£13,000	£31,000
Depreciation of equipment	£23,000	£15,000	£38,000
Total	£787,000	£580,000	£1,367,000

The unit cost per student learning hour was therefore:

Total overhead costs for the year / Total student learning hours for the year

=   £1,367,000 / 1,400,000

=   £0.98

In other words, it cost 98p in overheads every time a student spent an hour doing guided learning activities within the college.

Using this figure to calculate overheads for the Revive project, therefore:

There are 30 beneficiaries on the project, and each of them is expected to have 21 hours of guided learning per week (including advice and guidance) for 10 weeks. So the total student learning hours on the project are

30 beneficiaries x 21 hours per week x 10 weeks

=   6,300 student learning hours

The overhead per student learning hour is 98p, so the total overhead cost for the project is:

6,300 student learning hours x £0.98

=   £6,174

It is also common to apportion by the use of space within a building or by actual recorded usage of teaching rooms. All these methods require detailed records to be kept in relation to the factor used in the apportionment. For example, if apportioning by beneficiary hours you would need to be able to prove the number of hours spent by beneficiaries on the programme by keeping signing in and out sheets or registers. Apportionment by staff time requires staff to fill in time sheets to prove how many hours they have worked on the project. All this takes time and resources.

Many of these apportionment methods have been developed in response to the requirements of the European Social Fund (ESF) either through direct bidding or co-financing. As the ESF programme in the UK reduces in scale over the coming years, it is likely that complex apportionment methods will become less common as most other funds are less rigorous about how overheads are calculated. Carrying out an overhead calculation can still be a useful exercise, however, as many organisations are unaware of how much a project might be costing them. Underestimates of the level of overhead required can put a serious financial strain on an organisation and in the case of smaller organisations could lead to redundancies or even complete closure.

Funding issues

Different funds have different regulations about how money is to be managed and spent and obviously it is going to be essential to understand these in detail and stick to them. Although regulations vary from fund to fund, some terms and concepts crop up quite regularly. Perhaps the most common recurring concepts are those of **eligible expenditure** and **match funding,** each of which is covered in some detail below.

Eligible expenditure

The European Social Fund (including co-financing) is notorious for having strict regulations about what the money can be spent on and what it can't, though other funds can have similar restrictions too. For all grant funding, money can only be claimed back if it has been spent directly on the project, otherwise the claim could be fraudulent. The uncertainly lies in knowing where to draw the line around what is direct project expenditure and what isn't.

Consider the following examples:

1. The Human Resources Department of a large organisation makes a

charge to the project budget to cover the costs of the support they have given to the project team over the last year.

2. A consultant charges £500 a day for preparing a project claim.

3. After the project has officially finished, the project manager is asked to pay £8 each for beneficiaries to receive their qualification certificates.

4. The bank charges a small organisation an overdraft fee of £100.

Taking these examples one at a time:

1. This might be considered as eligible expenditure if the HR Department can provide proof of the amount of time they spent directly supporting the project. However, this proof can be hard to obtain as not everyone is prepared to complete time sheets (see Chapter 9 for more on monitoring). If a notional or estimated amount has been charged, some funders will be unwilling to pay for this.

2. Consultant fees are often a grey area. Most funds are prepared to pay for consultants to carry out essential specialist roles in relation to the actual content of the project, but not all will pay for consultants to carry out project management tasks such as completing claims. This becomes even more uncertain when consultants are engaged to write bids – few funders will pay for this.

3. A lot of funds have specific time limits within which the money must be spent. Any expenditure that occurs outside of this time limit cannot be refunded.

4. Not all funds will cover bank charges – the European Social Fund certainly won't.

As a general principle, funding from charitable trusts tends to be more flexible than big funds such as ESF or Lottery. However they may have different restrictions on funding, such as only paying for costs that are incurred by voluntary sector organisations, or only paying for staff costs. If in doubt it is always best to check directly with the funders.

Match funding

Match funding is a subject that strikes fear into many hearts, and for good reason! The principle behind match funding is simple – a fund pays for part of the cost of the project, the rest of the costs have to be found from a different source. If this sounds straightforward, be assured that the devil is in the detail. There are many operational difficulties with match funding. For example, if a project is drawing its money from two different funds, what if the two funds have different start and end dates? And which project outputs belong to which fund? How do you decide which fund pays for which costs?

Match funding doesn't always have to be in hard cash, it can be in kind – counting the cost of services or products supplied by one or more organisations that are involved in the project. All match funding that is supplied in kind needs to be given a monetary value so that it can be accounted for. With very few exceptions, the amount of match funding that is provided is based on the actual cost of the product or service to the organisation supplying it, not on any notional, estimated or commercial rate.

Case Study Example – Match Funding in Kind (Revive Project)

The project required 26 days of IT trainer time, and the college had agreed to provide this as part of their match funding. Initially the college Financial Controller had costed this as £400 per day, as this was the commercial rate at which the college had been selling its IT training staff to train local business people. This gave an estimated match funding of:

$$26 \times £400 = £10,400$$

However, the project manager soon realised that this would not stand up to an ESF audit because it cannot be traced back to actual costs incurred by the college in employing the IT trainer. The actual cost of employing the trainer, including on-costs, worked out as £111.62 per day. This gave a match funding of:

$$26 \times £111.62 = £2,909.12$$

The college, therefore, had to revise the funding of the project and make up the shortfall of match funding from elsewhere. This involved writing to both the Lottery and ESF secretariats to inform them of the change. Although this was a difficult process, not informing the funders of this change would have exposed the college to an unacceptable level of risk that if the project was audited, some of the funding would have to be returned. What is more, if the auditor suspected that the college had signed the match funding declaration knowing that the match funding had been wrongly calculated then this would open the college up to a charge of fraud.

Overestimating the amount of match funding available is a common reason for projects not being able to claim all their funding, though with the reduction in scale of the ESF programme in the UK this is becoming less of an issue because few other funds have such a strict match funding requirement.

Working with more than one funding stream

Many organisations work with a range of different funding streams and a particular area of work – even a particular project – may be funded from a range of sources. Keeping all the funders happy is not an easy job, especially as they might all have different requirements. However, in order to make the job manageable it is best if possible to develop one single system for financial management rather than trying to have separate systems for each fund. This will mean developing a system that meets the requirements of the strictest funder in terms of both financial management and monitoring and that is capable of surviving an audit. This theme will be developed more fully in Chapter 9.

Summary

The project budget forms one of the major constraints on any project. It is essential to estimate project costings accurately, as there may be little opportunity to make changes once the project has been approved.

There are two basic approaches to **estimating the staff costs** for a project: estimating based on **staff appointments**, and using the **project schedule**. In practice, many project managers use a combination of the two.

If estimating costs based on staff appointments, it is important to consider the level of responsibility that the new staff member will take and the range of their duties. There may be a standard pay scale within the occupational sector or the organisation. The amount of management time that will be required to supervise the new staff member should also be taken into account and included in the costings where possible.

Basing the staff budget on the project schedule involves adding up the number of staff hours, days or weeks from the schedule information. It is important also to include time for project management tasks as this is easily overlooked.

Other project costs may be simpler to estimate. However, you may be required to carry out an apportionment of **overhead costs** for the project. This involves adding up all the (eligible) overhead costs and dividing by some variable across the organisation such as 'number of staff days' or 'number of learning hours'

Some funds are stricter than others about financial management and tracking. The stricter funds will provide guidelines as to how the funding should be spent. This can create difficulties and uncertainties as the project progresses as there may be 'grey areas' in which a lot depends on how the spend is justified. Some funds also require that **match funding** is put in place, and that this is also spent in accordance with the guidelines.

Further reading

Construction project management in the voluntary sector:
www.sportengland.org/management-vol.pdf

CHAPTER EIGHT

Taking on a project part way through

You've taken over the running of a project part way through, or perhaps someone has written an ingenious and successful funding bid that you now have to turn into a workable project. There is little or no documentation. The bid is written in incomprehensible jargon. Your predecessor has vanished without a trace...

Where do you start?

Taking on a project at the early stages

If you've picked up a project fairly near the beginning of its life then things might be a little easier. You should have at your disposal some kind of bid or proposal, or at the very least someone who can talk you through the big idea. Your task is to turn vision into reality. This chapter gives you a step by step process that will help you to establish where you are and to make a plan to deliver the project successfully.

Taking on a project in its later stages

Depending on the state the project has been left in, you might be required to do a lot of research and possibly some replanning. This will vary depending on your circumstances. If a project plan does not exist, or if it is so out of date as to be useless, you may want to work right through this chapter and plan the project as if from scratch, but taking into account what, if anything, has already been achieved. In addition you will need to talk to everyone who has been involved in the project to date, including senior management, administrative staff, partners and steering group members.

Reading the bid

If the project is being funded by an external source, for example one of the major funding schemes, you are likely to be faced with a bid of some kind. This will detail the project in a way designed to appeal to those making the decision about funding.

Although most funding agencies will agree that they prefer bids to be written in a simple, straightforward style, many bids are still written in a language of their own, in which all is not quite as it seems! There are certain key words and phrases that seem to be a part of 'bid speak' that can be misleading or difficult to follow, and which make translating a funding bid into a workable project plan far from easy. Many funding agencies are just as guilty of introducing jargon within their own documentation too. The Jargon Buster in the Appendix goes through some of the words and phrases most commonly used by experienced bid writers and funding agencies and explains them in plain English.

Establishing the basics

Your first task is to draw out from the information at your disposal exactly where the project stands at this moment in time. Questions you may want to ask at this stage include:

How are we doing for time? It's not uncommon for a bid or proposal to be written assuming that the project will start right away. In reality it may take a while to gain approval for the project and, if externally funded, there may be a contract negotiation stage. Following this, if a project manager needs to be appointed this could mean a further delay of anything up to three months. Add in some management procrastination, and it might well turn out that you are being asked to deliver a project in about half the time that was originally planned for it. You will also need to check the ending date of the project – some deadlines are flexible but others, especially those set by funding bodies, can be rigid. In total, how much time do you have to deliver the project?

What has to be done? A project bid or proposal is likely to make very wide claims about the benefits of the project, but you will need to assess the bottom line. You will need to look at:

■ The outputs (or outcomes) – measurable achievements of the project that have been set. These could include the number of learners recruited to a project, number of businesses assisted, number of people achieving a qualification, number of people entering employment, number of pupils going on work placements etc. There may also be a list of 'soft outcomes' – achievements of the project that are more difficult to measure but are nonetheless important. These might include improved confidence among the beneficiary group, or a more positive approach to learning. Soft outcomes are just as important as hard outputs. The list of outputs and outcomes should tell you what you will need to do, but is unlikely to say how it should be done.

■ The aims and objectives – what do these boil down to? Aims should be very broad and strategic whereas objectives should be descriptions of what the project will achieve. At this stage, therefore, the objectives will be more useful to you and should provide some kind of backup to the outputs in telling you what needs to be achieved. Be aware when you read the documents that many people do not know the difference between aims and objectives!

■ Any particular requests by the funders. Some funders – particularly charitable trusts but sometimes larger bodies like the Learning and Skills Council too – will ask that targets are changed in some way, or that the proposal is refocused to help meet their own priorities better. If there have been any requests like this they should be in a letter or contract offer. You may want to contact the funders for further clarification if major changes have been requested.

How should it be done? Some projects have a very well worked out methodology that has been developed for good reasons, is based on experience in working with the target beneficiary group and fits with the overall approach of the organisation. Others, sad to say, have methodologies that have been given little thought other than to look impressive to whoever is assessing the bid or proposal. Projects such as this can turn out to be unworkable without a serious rethink. You will need to make a judgement on this based on talking the project through with those involved in writing the bid or proposal and your own experience. You will also need to take into account the time you have left to deliver the project, which could have a big influence on how things are done. The good news is that it's often much easier to make changes to the way a project is carried out than to change the outputs or budget.

How much money is available? This may require a little more than looking at the amount of funding that has been set aside or requested when the project was originally dreamed up, especially if the project is externally funded. Sometimes it is the case that funding bodies award a lower amount of money than was originally requested. It is worth asking questions about this, as this information may not be readily at hand. At the very least there should be some kind of letter confirming the amount of funding to be awarded and the schedule of payments. If this letter is not available you would be advised to contact the funding body yourself to obtain a copy.

Another factor that may affect the funding is the amount of time left to deliver the project. As was mentioned above, there may have been delays in starting the project and this could result in a potential saving in staff costs. If, for example, the project has budgeted for a full time project manager for one year but the project doesn't appoint a manager until there are only nine months to go, then there will be a saving equivalent to three months of salary. If the funder has not reduced the amount of funding awarded then this is good news because this money could potentially be spent elsewhere in the project, perhaps to bring in additional staff resources. Of course the bad news is that the whole project still has to be delivered in nine months!

Finally, you may need to take match funding into account. Match funding is defined in the Jargon Buster in the Appendix and is also discussed in Chapter 7. The implications to you at this stage of having a project that requires match funding are as follows:

- You will not receive funding equal to the total cost of the project – so check how much funding you will actually receive rather than looking at the total budget.

- Where is the match funding coming from? Has it been thought through? Is it being provided in cash from another funding source, or will it be provided in kind by relying on contributions of staff time and overheads from your own or a partner organisation?

- Your project may be receiving funds from more than one source – and each source could have slightly different regulations and timescales. Have all the sources of funding been confirmed or are some still awaiting a decision? How will you satisfy the requirements of each of the funders?

- If match funding is to be provided in kind, what will the in kind donation consist of? How will you account for it? Is it realistic, and can your organisation afford it?

Issues of funding, including match funding, are explored more deeply in Chapter 7.

Fixed points and negotiable points

All this information, in other words: **what** you have to do, **how** you have to do it, by **when** and for **how much** gives you a starting point for creating an action plan. As well as having an idea of the fixed, non-negotiable points within the project, you may also have an idea where there could be room for some negotiation.

Flexibility is most common in terms of how the project will be delivered. If the funding has been reduced there is also likely to be some flexibility in terms of what has to be delivered, as funders may be prepared to accept that less can be achieved if the funding has been cut, particularly if the cut is significant. Timescales can be flexible depending on the funding scheme – the larger funding schemes tend to have much less room for manoeuvre because timetables will be set by UK Government or the European Union. Finally, while it may be possible to negotiate a smaller budget it is rare to be able to negotiate a larger one.

A lot of this will depend on how the project is funded. Some funders, and some funding schemes, are more flexible than others. Although it varies considerably, charitable trusts can be very flexible as long as you consult them and keep them involved. (Of course there will be some exceptions to this rule!) Larger funding schemes such as the European Social Fund (ESF) and the various Lottery funds have the potential to be flexible but only within certain rules. The key here again is to consult with whoever is administering the funds, but you would be advised to learn as much about the regulations of the funding as possible before doing so.

You will also need to pay attention to the flexibility of your own organisation. Some organisations have a particular way of going about things and it may not be possible to negotiate. For example, some organisations are resistant to taking on casual or contract staff, something you may have planned to do in order to reduce the fixed staffing costs of the project. It would be worthwhile consulting a senior member of staff during the planning process, or at the very least running the plan past a senior manager once it has been prepared.

You may also find that there are certain expectations within the organisation about what this project will achieve and how. Some of these may be unrealistic, so it is doubly important to communicate with staff at all levels about the reality of the situation. If you are new to the organisation you may have to be a little cautious in introducing too many innovations at once. Discussing the project and your various options with individuals (especially those in senior positions) may help. But don't neglect the good news too. Stay positive, because you are there to ensure, somehow, that the project is a success and once you have a definite action plan you can use it to generate enthusiasm for the project and what it will achieve.

Making a plan

Once you have all the information at your fingertips you can start to plan the project – and in doing so see if it is still feasible. Chapter 2 goes into project planning in some detail, but here are some first considerations.

Firstly, although the buck stops with the project manager in terms of planning, it would be valuable to get the whole team involved. This could include staff internal to your own organisation such as administrators, finance staff, staff who will be working on the project (e.g. trainers, advisers, specialists) HR staff, and project partners. Ideally you should also include at least one representative from the targeted beneficiary group as well. In fact if the project is at a fairly early stage a management meeting or steering group could be convened to brainstorm and help to come up with a plan. For larger projects, especially those with many partners, an 'away day' may even be helpful.

A good place to start the process is to compare the outputs or outcomes you have to achieve, along with the way things are to be done, with the time available. For example if you have to run two cohorts of beneficiaries on a course of fifteen weeks each and have only twenty-six weeks left to do it, it's obvious that you are going to struggle unless you overlap the two and still leave some time to recruit to the course.

Similarly, if the budget has been cut you may find that things will have to change considerably. If the project relies on you recruiting, for example, a marketing adviser for £25,000 but the project budget has been cut to £20,000 you may have to think of other ways of going about things, perhaps by buying in expertise on an 'as required' basis. It can even be the case that the project manager finds that there is not enough money in the budget to pay their own salary! In extreme cases it may be necessary to go searching for other additional sources of funding.

The key is to think flexibly, and at every stage of planning to review the project, asking yourself:

- What has changed since the project was originally planned?
- Does the original methodology still allow us to meet the outputs within the required budget or timeframe?
- Is there any flexibility on the number and type of outputs?
- Are there other ways to meet the outputs?

This last point is perhaps where project staff and partners can give the most valuable input – and this can be done at any stage of the project as part of a replanning process as well as at the early stages.

You should then be able, using the information you have gathered about the project, to work through these ideas to see which could be taken forward. Chapter 2 will give you the tools and techniques you need to turn these ideas into a fully worked-up project plan.

Communicate the plan

As has been mentioned, it is important to communicate what you intend to do with staff directly involved in the project, with project partners and with wider staff in your own organisation. Ideally they should have been involved in generating a plan of action in the first place, at least to the extent of contributing ideas, experience and points of view.

It is also of vital importance to talk through the proposed plan with a representative of whoever is funding the project. If the project is funded internally to the organisation then this step has already been covered, but if, as is more common, the funding is external then you will need to find an appropriate way of letting the funders know of any proposed changes.

How this is done will depend on the funding organisation and the scheme or fund under which the project is running. Some funders (for example, Government Offices) ask for a letter detailing any significant changes. Others, while they eventually need to see something in writing, will be prepared to talk things over with you. This is particularly the case where your project has been assigned a contract manager.

When discussing your proposed way forward, you should be prepared for some or part of your ideas to be rejected. However, if this is the case then press the funders to be allowed to talk it over with someone. You may be able to reach a workable compromise, or indeed you might find that the funding organisation comes up with some good ideas that hadn't occurred to you. Organisations providing or administering funding themselves have to report back on their success, so it will be in their interests to help you succeed to the best of their ability.

Checklist: Taking on a project

At what stage are you taking on the project?

What information is available to you, and where can you find it?

How much time is left?

What needs to be achieved?

How will the project be carried out?

How much funding is available?

What are the expectations within your own organisation?

What are the fixed points and what are the negotiable points of the project?

Who should be involved in devising a new plan?

Who should you inform of the completed plan?

How are you going to ensure that this project succeeds?

CHAPTER NINE

Project monitoring and evaluation

Having spent a great deal of time creating and perfecting a project plan it is tempting to think that all will therefore go according to the plan. Unfortunately, this never seems to be the case in project management and any number of unforeseen circumstances can take the project off track. The very worst thing you can do with a project plan – especially the schedule which probably represents a great deal of work – is treat it with too much reverence. Putting it on the wall is just as bad as putting it away in a drawer. It is a working document, a tool that needs to be used if it is to have any value.

The key is to build in ways to use the plan – at review meetings, once a week on a Monday morning, as part of meetings with the project team or partners. This will allow everyone to see whether the project is still on track or if it has gone awry. If things have gone wrong, you can then decide what action needs to be taken. This is the essence of project **monitoring**. The first part of this chapter takes a detailed look at monitoring, how it can be used to ensure that the project stays on track and does what it set out to do. The second part of the chapter turns its attention to **evaluation** which draws on research as well as monitoring information to assess how well the project has met its stated aims and objectives. Evaluation can be used to judge the effectiveness of a project, and can also be used as a learning opportunity for those working on the project and others involved in similar work.

Tolerance

In all projects there needs to be some flexibility to cope with change, but there comes a point at which change becomes the first step towards failure and the project manager needs to be able to work out at what point this happens. **Tolerance** is the amount of change that is allowable if the project is still to be successful. This can be calculated for any of the attributes of a project:

- Time
- Money
- Outcomes.

The tolerance limits for a project may be set by the funder. For example, some funders ask to be notified with a revised plan if the project deviates in money or outcomes by a certain percentage – say 10% or 15%. Even if this is not required by funders, it is a useful approach and the percentage tolerance can be altered to suit the nature of the project and how critical it is to stick closely to the plan. This can be calculated over the whole project or, perhaps more usefully, at set points during the project, say quarterly or monthly.

Thus a project can be monitored at its simplest level by comparing the planned spend and outcomes against the actual spend and outcomes on a regular basis.

Case Study – Youth Volunteering Project

The Youth Volunteering Project was set up in a small market town to encourage young people to engage productively with their local community by volunteering for a wide range of environmental and social projects. This was a small project that had been given a grant by the local Parish Council. The project manager had submitted a monthly spend profile to the Parish Council and as the project progressed was able to monitor actual spend against this profile. Eight months into the project, the monitoring record was as follows:

Month	Planned spend	Actual spend	% Difference
January	£100	£91.20	-9%
February	£300	£267.00	-11%
March	£450	£295.00	-34%
April	£160	£184.50	15%
May	£50	£43.50	-13%
June	£50	£42.10	-16%
July	£50	£58.40	17%
August	£50	£49.20	-2%
September	£50		
October	£50		
November	£50		
December	£50		

The percentage difference was calculated by subtracting the planned spend from the actual spend and dividing this by the planned spend. This was then converted into a percentage by multiplying by 100.

The project manager had agreed to inform the Parish Council if the spend varied by more than 20% in any one month, or overall. She therefore notified the Chair of the Parish Council that the project had underspent by 34% during March, and provided a short rationale for this.

By November, it became clear that the project overall was not going to spend all its allocated money. In fact the actual spend for September, October and November had been £45 each month. This meant that the total actual spend up to November was £1,165.90. The total amount that had been allocated to the project was £1,410 – so in December the project would have to spend £244.60 to use up all the allocated money and this was not going to happen.

The project manager in the case study had known she was underspending most months but hadn't realised how much this was adding up to overall until it was too late. What she could have done was to track her **cumulative** spend over the project. This means comparing what she had spent so far each month, compared to what she should have spent so far. This would have given a clearer picture of how the project overall was going, in terms of its finances.

The table below shows how this could have been done.

Month	Allocated spend	Cumulative allocated spend	Actual spend	Cumulative actual spend
January	£100	£100	£91.20	£91.20
February	£300	£400	£267.00	£358.20
March	£450	£850	£295.00	£653.20
April	£160	£1,010	£184.50	£837.70
May	£50	£1,060	£43.50	£881.20
June	£50	£1,110	£42.10	£923.30
July	£50	£1,160	£58.40	£981.70
August	£50	£1,210	£49.20	£1,030.90
September	£50	£1,260		
October	£50	£1,310		
November	£50	£1,360		
December	£50	£1,410		

This shows that the overall actual spend starts to fall away from the allocated spend by March and never catches up in the subsequent months, so as early as March the project manager could have seen that the project was not running to plan.

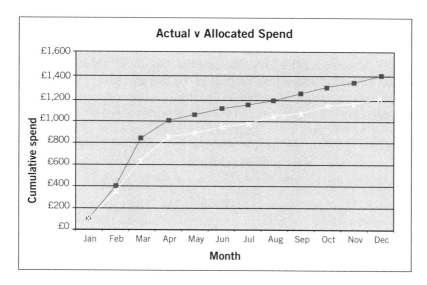

The graph above illustrates the difference between the actual and allocated spend and shows very clearly that things started to go wrong in March.

This same approach could be used for measuring the difference between predicted and actual outcomes, especially where a project includes a large number of countable outcomes like number of people trained or number of businesses informed.

Sometimes not spending all the allocated funding is not a problem and might be the result of astute cost savings along the way. More often lack of spend is a sign that the project is going wrong somehow and this is certainly the case if the outcomes are not being achieved.

Project time is not tracked in the same way, and this is where the project schedule can help. If a project is slipping in time then tasks will not be started and completed by the dates given in the schedule, and the schedule will need updating. It is vital to carry out a regular update of the schedule if dates start slipping at all because otherwise there is nothing to work to and no plan for getting the project back on track. It is perhaps easy to put this off, or to think that you will catch up somehow. In fact in practice this is what the majority of us do to some degree! But optimism is misplaced in such situations and in order for the project to achieve its potential it needs to be forced back on track, however painful this process may be. This will involve reviewing the whole project, perhaps working out different ways to achieve the outcomes or bringing in additional people or partners, and **rescheduling**. Rescheduling, as the name suggests, means redrawing all or part of the project schedule using revised information.

A full reschedule is not always necessary. Scrutiny of the schedule will give a clue as to whether the time slippage is one that can easily be fixed or if a more serious rethink is required. In Chapter 2 we saw how the critical path of a project contained all the tasks that had to be completed strictly on time in order for the project to succeed. This is helpful in terms of monitoring because if tasks that are not on the critical path are slipping then it may be possible to make up the time elsewhere, whereas if the critical path tasks are the ones that are affected then this is a more serious issue.

Even if you have not been able to produce a full PERT chart for the project (not easy without using project management software) a table of tasks and dependencies (Chapter 2) should provide enough information to know which tasks are time critical. Sometimes this will be obvious anyway, without this level of analysis.

A systematic approach to dealing with time slippage is given in the flowchart opposite.

As you will notice, any slippage in the project schedule has potentially serious consequences, including adding to the costs in most cases. Most funders are unwilling to pay additional costs and so it is likely that these would have to be absorbed somehow by the organisation. Because of this it is far too easy to ignore project slippage and hope for the best rather than face up to the consequences, but the longer a problem is ignored the bigger it tends to grow. It is much better to make smaller changes along the way, painful as these might be, than to store up a big problem for the last few months of the project when it may be too late to make any positive changes anyway.

Some organisations are more hostile to changes in a project than others and management may be tempted to see any revisions to the schedule or changes to the budget as a sign of failure. It is perhaps a difficult message to have to convey, but making changes to keep the project on track is in fact a sign of **good** project management. It is good practice to keep

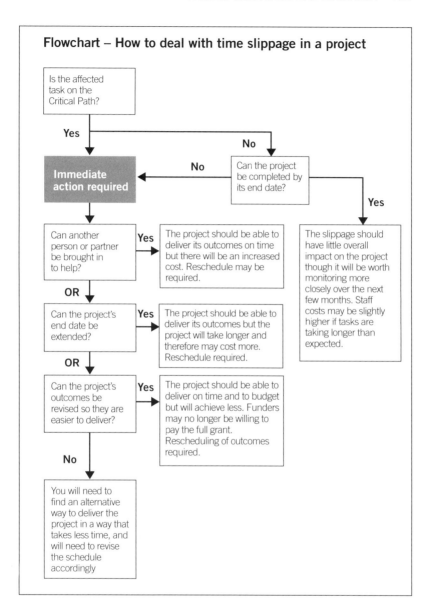

Flowchart – How to deal with time slippage in a project

Is the affected task on the Critical Path?

Yes

No

Can the project be completed by its end date?

No

Immediate action required

Yes

Can another person or partner be brought in to help?

Yes → The project should be able to deliver its outcomes on time but there will be an increased cost. Reschedule may be required.

OR

Can the project's end date be extended?

Yes → The project should be able to deliver its outcomes but the project will take longer and therefore may cost more. Reschedule required.

OR

Can the project's outcomes be revised so they are easier to deliver?

Yes → The project should be able to deliver on time and to budget but will achieve less. Funders may no longer be willing to pay the full grant. Rescheduling of outcomes required.

No

You will need to find an alternative way to deliver the project in a way that takes less time, and will need to revise the schedule accordingly

The slippage should have little overall impact on the project though it will be worth monitoring more closely over the next few months. Staff costs may be slightly higher if tasks are taking longer than expected.

managers up to date with the progress of the project, including slippage and underspend, though this may not make you popular. Steering group members could prove good allies if the going gets rough, especially if they have been involved in the monitoring of the project.

Quality monitoring

Monitoring is not just a question of ensuring that the project meets its aims and objectives, it also has a role in ensuring the quality of delivery. This may include, for example:

■ Extent to which the project has met its equality of opportunity targets

■ How learner-centred any training, advice or guidance has been

■ Level of support offered to volunteers

■ Inclusivity of committees or steering group.

Depending on the nature of the project, there could be many other aspects that need monitoring throughout to ensure that it is delivered to the right quality. Some of these may already be dealt with through other means – for example the quality of training might be monitored on an organisation-wide basis by the Adult Learning Inspectorate or a similar body. Other things will be more specific to the project, such as the extent to which the project is recruiting from the group it set out to target.

Case Study – Trade Training

Trade Training was a project that aimed to target black and minority ethnic (BME) businesses in a large city and offer both the business owners and their employees expert consultancy and relevant short training courses that would help their businesses survive and grow.

The project had set targets that all of the thirty businesses it set out to help would be owned and managed by people from BME communities. Within this it set out to support four businesses within the Turkish community and four businesses from the Nigerian community, as these were significant communities in the area with a high business start-up rate but which were statistically far less likely to access business support services than average.

The project was to run for eighteen months and the steering group met at the beginning of the project and every six months afterwards.

At the second meeting of the steering group it was reported that five businesses had been supported, with three of these being BME businesses and none from either the Turkish or Nigerian communities. Using this information, the steering group was able to emphasise to the project manager that enquiries from non-BME SMEs should be referred to other projects in the area, as this project was specifically for BME businesses. Furthermore, it suggested that greater efforts be made to reach the Turkish and Nigerian communities, perhaps by identifying and working with leaders from these communities.

At the third meeting, one year into the project, the project manager reported that twelve further businesses had been supported. All of these were BME businesses, and three were from the Nigerian community. None were from the Turkish community. The steering group consulted with a member of the Turkish community in the area, who told them that there was already some business support, both formal and informal, within the local Turkish community. However, he suspected there may be other factors that were putting people off getting involved in formal business support outside the community and that this was of concern.

After some discussion it was agreed that the project was not specialised enough to offer the required support to the Turkish community and the project was re-profiled to include support for six Nigerian community businesses but none specifically from the Turkish community. The funder was consulted and agreed to this change.

As a result, the partnership involved decided to develop an action research project aimed at understanding and responding to the needs of the Turkish business community, working in partnership with a small Turkish business association and employing a Turkish speaking development worker.

As the example above illustrates, it is easy to drift from the original project targets in the day to day running of the project, and sometimes to risk missing the point of the project altogether even though, on paper, targets are being met. Regular monitoring, especially where overseen by an objective eye such as a steering group, can help maintain the focus of the project and ensure that it meets its aims as well as its objectives. Another point illustrated by the example is that such monitoring is only worthwhile if the results are acted upon.

Equal opportunities monitoring should of course have a much broader scope than ethnicity and will cut through all aspects of the project. Chapter 4 provides more detail on diversity and equality of opportunity. Another aspect of quality that may be monitored throughout the project is beneficiary focus. For training projects, this will include how learner-centred the project is – for example, do learners have individual learning plans, do learners have an opportunity to comment on the quality and relevance of their teaching, is there a structured follow-up of all leavers and so on. For all types of project, this might include how involved beneficiaries are in decision making (are they represented on the steering group?) and how feedback is gathered and followed up.

Keeping monitoring records

Maintaining records to help with monitoring should not be a mere paper exercise, even though some of these records will be necessary in the case of an audit. It is an unfortunate fact that we tend to concentrate on what we measure. If the record keeping system serves the project and underpins its aims and objectives then it is an essential support that ensures the project is achieved on time, to budget and to the required quality. If record keeping is not viewed in this way it can easily mushroom into a bureaucracy.

A system for maintaining records needs to be thought through as early as possible – before the project begins is ideal although this may not always be feasible. The questions to ask at this stage – and do involve as many other people as possible in this process, including partners – include:

- What do we need to know to ensure that the project runs to plan?
- What do we need to know to maintain the quality of the project?

The first stage to drawing up a monitoring system is to think through the different categories of records you will need to keep.

Case Study Example – Youth Volunteering Project Monitoring System (1)

The Youth Volunteering project detailed above required the project manager to keep clear and auditable records to provide feedback to the Parish Council. The project manager also wished to maintain records that would help to ensure that the project was meeting its original aims and objectives. A short discussion with a colleague resulted in the following diagram:

This summarised the areas of monitoring information that the project manager needed to keep during the course of the project.

At this stage the categories are very broad and although the case study deals with a small project this would also be the case for larger projects. The next step is to break this down into more detail, and to specify exactly what information needs to be recorded in each of these categories.

Case Study Example – Youth Volunteering Project Monitoring System (2)

The project manager drew up the following table to summarise the data that needed to be recorded in each of the above categories. For each item of information she detailed why these records were being kept. This is a very useful exercise that can prevent unnecessary bureaucracy.

Category	Reason
Information about volunteers:	
Name	In order to be able to count the overall number of volunteers
Age	To show that the project is targeting the appropriate age group
Ethnicity	To demonstrate effective equal opportunities practice
Gender	As above
Disability status	As above
Address (including postcode)	To ensure good geographical coverage of the project and highlight any issues relating to geographical inaccessibility
Type of placement sought	To demonstrate that young people's preferences were taken into account when setting up a volunteer placement
Name and address of placement	As above
Project management information:	
Information about volunteer placements:	
Financial details:	

Only the first part of the table is completed in this example, but in reality the project manager completed the whole table.

The left hand column in a table such as this will give you a complete picture of all the information you will need to collect in order to monitor effectively, but monitoring information is never collected on a piece-by-piece basis. Instead it is collected at intervals on forms, as reports, on official documentation such as invoices and receipts and so on. The challenge therefore is to design a system that will allow these individual pieces of information to be collected in the most efficient manner possible.

This will involve looking at the overall picture rather than category by category, as you may find that there is some overlap in the information needed for each of your categories. For example, in the Youth Volunteering

Project, the name and address of the volunteer placements was required in the 'Information about volunteers' category and in the 'information about volunteer placements' category.

Case Study Example – Youth Volunteering Project Monitoring System (3)

The project manager drew up two forms, one to be completed by potential young volunteers as they first became involved with the project and one to be completed by placement organisations when they were preparing to take one or more volunteers. These forms contained all the information required in the two categories, and provided a means by which the placements could be cross-referenced with the volunteers.

Youth Volunteering Project Volunteer Registration Form

1. Personal Details

Forename(s) _____ Surname _____

Address _____

_____ Postcode _____

Date of Birth __/__/__   Are you: Male ☐ Female ☐

2. Equal Opportunities Monitoring

Which of the following groups do you consider you belong to?

Asian or Asian British – Bangladeshi ☐	Mixed – White and Asian ☐
Asian or Asian British – Indian ☐	Mixed – White and Black African ☐
Asian or Asian British – Pakistani ☐	Mixed – White and Black Caribbean ☐
Asian or Asian British – Other ☐	Mixed – Other ☐
Black or Black British – African ☐	White – British ☐
Black or Black British – Caribbean ☐	White – Irish ☐
Black or Black British – Other ☐	White – Other ☐
Chinese ☐	Other ☐
Prefer not to say ☐	

Do you have a disability?

Yes ☐   No ☐   Prefer not to say ☐

3. Placement type

Please indicate the type of placement that would interest you:

☐ Working with children and young people
☐ Working with the elderly
☐ Working with people who have a physical disability
☐ Working with animals
☐ Conservation work
☐ Office work (filing, photocopying etc.)

Other (please give details) _____

Which days/times are you available for volunteer work? _____

4. Declaration

I declare that the details given on this form are true to the best of my knowledge.

Signed _____ Date _____

▶

Placement Registration Form: Youth Volunteering Project

Name of organisation ——————————————————

Address ——————————————————————

Legal status ——————————————————————

Named contact ————————————————————

Telephone ——————————————————————

Do you have a published health and safety policy? ——————

Who will be responsible for ensuring the health and safety of volunteers (name and contact details)?

_____

Do you have a published equal opportunities policy? ——————

Who will be responsible for ensuring that good practice in equal opportunities is followed (name and contact details)?

_____

Do you have appropriate liability insurance?——————————

Signed: ——————————————————————

Date: ——————————————————————

Name(s) of volunteer(s) ——————————————————

The project manager also provided each placement organisation with a standard signing-in sheet to maintain a record of volunteer attendance and to comply with health and safety good practice.

Part way through the project, the Chair of the Parish Council became convinced that young people from outside the parish were giving false addresses in order to take part in the project, as they were keen to take advantage of the travel allowances paid to volunteers. The project manager did not think this was the case but was unable to prove it. She therefore carried out a check of a random sample of 20% of the volunteers, asking them to provide proof of address. She countersigned their registration forms to show that this had been done. None of the sample had given a false address, and this satisfied the Parish Council that there was probably nothing to worry about.

Not all information required for monitoring will need to be collected directly, some of it will already exist elsewhere in the organisation or will be held by partner organisations. Financial information often falls into this category as finance staff or departments will already maintain records. For some projects, beneficiary information will already exist, for example if the project takes place with school pupils, or in a college or university, or if the beneficiaries are already registered for an existing service. However, this information may not necessarily be adequate to meet the project's monitoring needs.

Cautionary Tale – IT Technician Training (based on a true story!)

A Technical College ran a fifteen-week IT technician training programme. All fifty of the beneficiaries were registered as students through the college's central systems by a team based at a different campus from the one at which the training took place. The project had no overall manager and the students were 'infilled' with fee-paying students on one of three courses that were being offered at the time. Because the beneficiaries had to fill in a registration form to enrol as a student, staff at the college did not ask them to fill in a separate beneficiary registration form and it was assumed that all was in order.

Nine months after the project had finished, the college was audited on several of its grant-funded projects, including IT Technician Training. The auditors quickly picked up that there was no record of the employment status of the beneficiaries on the day they started on the project. This was a serious omission because only those who had been unemployed for six months or more were eligible beneficiaries under the terms of the funding.

Staff at the college were asked to provide the missing information, but this proved difficult as the beneficiaries had now left the college and were difficult to contact. Only eight of the fifty beneficiaries were willing and able to provide proof that they had been unemployed for more than six months when the project started. While attempting to gather this evidence, college staff began to suspect that the marketing and recruitment had not been carried out properly and that some of the beneficiaries had not been eligible after all.

▶

> The auditors were able to take into account only the eight
> beneficiaries for whom proof could be provided, and therefore the
> project appeared to have under-recruited significantly and as a
> result was ordered to pay back the majority of the grant.

The above example illustrates, above all, how important it is for one person
to take responsibility for drawing up and implementing a monitoring
system. If responsibility is shared then there is a danger that the system
will be incomplete, with potentially serious consequences either in terms
of quality or auditability. This is exacerbated when more than one
department (or organisation) holds necessary records. It also demonstrates
that ongoing monitoring and review during the life of the project are more
than just administrative exercises, they are vital to the wellbeing of the
project and need to be taken seriously.

Maintaining records legally – The Data Protection Act

The Data Protection Act 1998 gives individuals rights over the personal
information that is held about them. This includes facts about individuals
such as name, gender and ethnicity, health records, training records and
so on. Most projects that work with individuals will therefore be affected
by the Data Protection Act.

At the core of the Act are eight principles of good practice. These state that
data must be:

1. Fairly and lawfully processed

2. Processed for limited purposes

3. Adequate, relevant and not excessive

4. Accurate

5. Not kept for longer than is necessary

6. Processed in line with your rights

7. Secure

8. Not transferred to countries without adequate protection.

There are various conditions under which data can be considered 'fairly processed'. The simplest of these is that the individual has given their consent for the data to be held and processed, although there are other conditions that would also constitute fair processing. However, when 'sensitive data' is involved, including ethnic origin, it is a requirement that an individual must have given their explicit consent for this data to be held.

This means that for many projects, the best way to ensure compliance with the Data Protection Act is to make it clear to individuals how data about them will be stored and processed and ask them to sign to show their consent.

Individuals have certain rights under law relating to the data that is held about them. These include the right to see the data that is held about them on computer records (including any record of people's opinions about them), and the right to require that data about them is corrected or deleted if inaccurate.

Most organisations will have a Data Protection policy and it is advisable to talk to someone within the organisation to ensure that the project complies with the Act. Further information can be found on the website of the Information Commissioner:

www.informationcommissioner.gov.uk

Evaluation strategy

Evaluation and monitoring are often linked together and indeed in some contexts there can be little difference between the two. The purpose of evaluation is to assess the project against its stated aims, objectives and other targets in order to provide meaningful feedback. Monitoring performs a similar role in tracking the project during its lifetime against its aims, objectives and constraints (time, money and outcome) to make sure it is on track. However, the concerns of evaluation are generally wider and may encompass not just the project but also the wider context and future work of the project partners.

Many people think of evaluation as something that takes place at the end of the project, providing a snapshot of how successful the project has been. This is **summative** evaluation, and is often quantitative in focus. **Formative** evaluation on the other hand seeks to inform the project throughout its life (and the development of future projects) by providing evidence, feedback and details of lessons learned. Both may draw heavily on monitoring information but may also include other sources of information, both qualitative and quantitative, including commissioned or participatory research.

The ideal time to plan a strategy for evaluation is at the outset of the project, asking of yourself, your project team and project partners what you would hope to get out of the process of evaluation. If the project is trying out something very new, or if the project is a short one, then the most important concern might be whether or not it worked. In this case it will be enough to concentrate on summative evaluation, and it will be necessary to put in place the processes that will record the information to answer this question. As well as standard monitoring information about, for example, the take-up of services on the project, this could include feedback questionnaires from beneficiaries, minutes of 'user group' meetings, or perhaps a longer term piece of commissioned research on impact. For other projects it may be preferable to focus attention on the more formative aspects of evaluation, drawing on information that will allow the project to grow and develop, and to record the lessons learned by practitioners as they go through the process of delivering the project.

The tools and techniques for carrying out an evaluation are many and varied and will draw heavily on the research tools discussed in Chapter 1. There have been many different approaches put forward and a wide range of tools developed, most of which can be found online through a basic web search. However, tools and techniques alone do not make for a good evaluation. As with many things in the world of project management, the best results are obtained through good planning and setting in place a coherent process that is both appropriate to and embedded within your project.

Evaluation, like research, starts with a question or a set of questions to which you are seeking answers. The tools and techniques selected should be capable of giving you an answer to these questions. Furthermore, they should be part of a process of feedback that will be used and reviewed throughout the life of the project, either by the project manager, the project team, the steering group or some other element of the project management structure.

An evaluation should ideally seek to be **inclusive**, taking into account the perspectives of a wide group of stakeholders such as beneficiaries, partners, the project team, perhaps the funders, and anyone else to whom the evaluation will be meaningful. The reasons for this are perhaps obvious but worth stating anyway. If your evaluation is to answer questions about whether the project was successful, then success may mean different things to different stakeholders and only an evaluation that has been planned to take multiple perspectives into account will genuinely provide an answer.

Above all, an evaluation should be useful and should be used. It takes a lot of time and expense to conduct a good evaluation of a project and this is wasted effort if, as often happens, the evaluation report is put into a drawer and never referred to again. It is worthwhile to plan, right from the outset, how the evaluation material will be used. If a report is published, what plans are there to disseminate its conclusions? Will they be presented at events or conferences, published as articles, summarised on a website? Are there policies in place to use previous evaluation results to inform the development of new projects, whether in the same team or elsewhere in the organisation? Thinking through these questions may raise larger questions about policy within the whole organisation, such as how knowledge is captured within the context of projects and how learning from projects across the organisation (or partnership) is used formally in the development of new projects. Such a knowledge management policy will help to ensure that mistakes are never repeated and that staff build on the experience gained not just by themselves and their immediate team but also on others right across the organisation.

An evaluation framework

There are many approaches to evaluation, some of which have been designed for specific types of project and others that are more general. Each project has to find an evaluation approach and methodology that best meets their needs, perhaps taking into account organisational policy, the needs of the funder and the organisational sector which may have its own standards and norms. If, however, there is no guidance or precedent available it will be up to the project manager to propose how the evaluation should take place. The framework below provides a starting point. It gives a general approach to evaluation that can be adapted and used by most projects:

1. **Questions:** Evaluation questions will usually centre around the extent to which the project met its aims and objectives and what was learned from carrying out the project. Formulate these at the outset of the project and agree them with as many people involved in the project as possible.

2. **Resources:** Gain agreement at an early stage about who will be

responsible for carrying out the evaluation and what resources they will have at their disposal.

3. **Tools:** Select the tools that will provide the data required for the evaluation. Some of the data is likely to be derived from existing (or proposed) monitoring systems.

4. **Process:** Set up processes to embed the evaluation within the day-to-day running of the project so that collection of evaluation data becomes part of the routine of project work.

5. **Analysis:** At set points (for example at the mid and end points of the project) analyse the data to derive meaningful conclusions.

6. **Dissemination:** Collate the evaluation material into a report or other similar format and disseminate to the widest possible audience.

7. **Ongoing use:** Use the lessons learned from the project to inform future project development.

Evaluation tools

Many of the tools that are used for evaluation, such as survey questionnaires, analysis of statistics or focus groups, are covered in Chapter 1 as they are general research techniques. Other approaches are more specific to evaluation and are detailed below.

Outcomes and indicators

Often within a project there are **outcomes** that you will want to measure or evaluate that don't lend themselves to a simple, quantitative approach. For example, a key outcome of a project may be that the beneficiaries increase their confidence, but how do you measure a change in someone's confidence? You could ask them in an interview as part of a questionnaire if they feel more confident, and that would provide you with some information. The problem is that the people you ask may find it difficult to remember how they felt before the start of the project, you might be asking them on a particularly good or bad day, or in some cases they may not understand the question, at least in the way you meant it. This is where **indicators** can help.

An indicator, as its name suggests, provides an indication that a change is taking place and is more easily measured. Indicators can be used to demonstrate that an outcome is being reached even if the outcome cannot be measured directly. Indicators should have some kind of logical link with the outcome in order to be valid. For example, an increase in confidence can manifest itself in a number of ways. Someone who has been out of work for a long time might demonstrate an increase in confidence by applying for more jobs or starting a course. These are things that can be measured and a project that was working with unemployed people might use the number of jobs applied for during a set period of time, say a week, as an indicator. Because this is something that can be counted, it can be compared against the number applied for in the week before the project started and a change can be shown.

A potential drawback of this approach is that the link between the outcome and the indicator may be difficult to prove. In our example above, a number of different factors other than confidence may be contributing to the number of jobs a person applies for. Perhaps an increased knowledge of the job market is more critical, for example. One way around this is to use multiple indicators that point towards the same outcome.

Case Study – Return to Work project

The Return to Work project was aimed at women who had been out of the labour market for more than two years because they were caring for children. In a similar previous project, many of the beneficiaries had mentioned that the project had greatly increased their confidence in all aspects of life as well as in relation to the workplace. The project team wanted to find a systematic way of capturing and measuring this change in confidence as a way of proving the worth of the project to potential funders.

The team commissioned a researcher to design a short questionnaire that would ask beneficiaries very specific questions about their level of confidence in particular situations. Beneficiaries would be asked to fill in the questionnaire at the beginning and the end of the project in order to compare the two sets of answers.

The questionnaire asked respondents to read a number of statements and to indicate how true the statements were for them on a scale of 1 – 10. Questions included:

- I feel happy about standing up and speaking in front of a small group of people

- I think I perform well in job interviews

- If I disagree with someone I am able to tell them so.

In the example above, the project team brought in researchers to devise the questionnaires. This ensured that the questions were carefully planned and worded in order to give the best and most reliable measure of confidence possible.

After Action Review

A simple but useful approach to formative evaluation is to carry out an After Action Review after an event or task within a project. This is a short document, often no more than one page, that summarises the lessons learned from the task. The review can be as elaborate or concise as is required, but usually contains sections on what worked well, what didn't work as well, what could be done differently and a plan of action for the future. This perhaps seems like a lot of extra work, but there are a number of reasons why it is a worthwhile exercise:

- You are unlikely to remember all the lessons learned from a task without writing them down, and far less likely to put changes into place

- Other people can benefit more easily from what you have learned if you write it down

- The review can include multiple perspectives by inviting contributions from the team, partners and beneficiaries

- If you leave and the project is taken over by someone else, it will prevent them making the same mistakes

Learning History

This is similar to an After Action Review but much more elaborate and better suited to evaluating a larger sequence of tasks or a whole project. It always includes multiple perspectives and is often facilitated by external evaluators. A Learning History consists of a series of narratives about the project or part of the project being evaluated, and these are analysed and commentated upon in order to draw out useful lessons. A Learning History may be a useful alternative approach to evaluation for a project that has been groundbreaking or unique. More about Learning Histories can be found on the website of the Learning History Research Project based at MIT: ccs.mit.edu/lh

Summary

A project can be monitored throughout its life to check whether it is on track in terms of time, money and outcomes. **Tolerance** is the amount of change that is acceptable before action needs to be taken. Tolerance limits can apply both to monthly or quarterly spend and achievements, and to **cumulative** totals.

A project experiencing time **slippage** in relation to tasks in its critical path is in immediate danger of failure. Although difficult both to implement and communicate, corrective action taken at an early stage can help to prevent a larger scale problem later on.

Quality aspects of projects can also be monitored in order to track how a project is performing against the standards it has set itself. These may include aspects of equality and diversity, inclusivity, beneficiary participation and feedback and so on.

A systematic approach to record keeping is essential to monitoring, but the system should serve the monitoring needs rather than vice versa. This requires a strategic and planned approach to monitoring that will allow a system to be developed that will collect all the required information in a practical and timely fashion. Where some of the required information is collected elsewhere in the organisation or partnership, these systems should be checked to ensure that they satisfy the project's monitoring requirements.

Monitoring and data collection systems should be checked to ensure they comply with the **Data Protection Act**.

Evaluation assesses the project against its aims and objectives to provide feedback on the extent to which it is meeting them. This can be used to answer questions about the effectiveness of the project and also to provide learning and development opportunities for those involved in the project. An effective evaluation should be planned right from the start of a project.

An evaluation may be **summative** or **formative**, or both. It may draw on both **quantitative** and **qualitative** techniques. Evaluation begins with a question or set of questions and uses tools to gather the data needed to answer those questions. The data is then analysed to give a set of conclusions and this information should be disseminated and used to improve the performance of current and future projects.

Many general research techniques such as questionnaires, interviews and focus groups can be used as part of an evaluation strategy. Some outcomes are more easily evaluated indirectly, using indicators. **After Action Reviews** and **Learning Histories** are tools derived from Knowledge Management that can be used as part of a formative evaluation strategy.

Further reading

Evaluating Development Projects was developed for the Higher Education sector, but is a useful general guide to evaluation strategy: www.dfes.gov.uk/dfee/heqe/projeval.htm

Outcomes and indicators are covered in detail in the paper Guide to Measuring Soft Outcomes and Distance Travelled: esf.gov.uk/_docs/distance[1].pdf

A comprehensive, though heavily academic, resource on evaluation is: Guba, E.G. and Lincoln, Y.S. (1989) *Fourth Generation Evaluation*. London, Sage.

Jargon buster

What it says	What it means
Added value	This describes how a project will achieve successes over and above those that would have been achieved without the project funding. It is most relevant where project funding is providing **match funding** to an existing activity funded through another source, thus allowing extra **outputs** to be achieved. However, it can sometimes be used in the context of describing how project funding will allow additional activity to take place over and above that which an organisation could fund from its own core resources.
Additionality	Additionality is a term often used interchangeably with **added value**. It is more often used in the context of large funding programmes, and is a core criterion of the European Social Fund (ESF). It is also a term used to flag up the fact that the ESF cannot be used to replace public funds that would normally be spent, or to allow public funds to be diverted elsewhere.
Barriers to progression/learning/ employment	The language of 'overcoming barriers' is very often used in the bidding world. The theory is that **beneficiaries** face a number of identifiable barriers to achieving the outcomes they want to achieve, such as education or employment, and that these barriers can be overcome by actions taken by the project team. This view clearly makes for a positive and coherent bid, but the reality is likely to be more complex.
Basic skills	The Basic Skills Agency defines basic skills as *'The ability to read, write and speak in English / Welsh and to use mathematics at a level necessary to function and progress at work and in society in general'*. The DfES have defined National Standards for literacy and numeracy at Entry Level and Levels 1 & 2 of the **national qualifications framework**. More information can be found at: www.dfes.gov.uk/readwriteplus/teachingandlearning
Beneficiaries	Beneficiaries are those directly benefiting from the activities of a project – those that you might call clients, students or learners.
BME	BME is short for Black and Minority Ethnic. It is used as a blanket term for groups of people that are not of white British origin.

What it says	What it means
Capital project/funding	Capital projects involve investing in buildings or equipment. Some kinds of funding will not support capital projects.
Co-financing	The European Social Fund (ESF) always requires **match funding** of up to 55%. Via a co-financing scheme, a project can request both the ESF money and the match funding in cash from an intermediary organisation such as the Learning and Skills Council (LSC) or Jobcentre Plus.
Community enterprise	A community enterprise is a venture that produces profit or other benefit for a whole community, or group(s) within a community, rather than for one or more individuals. The term **social enterprise** is now more often used, though this tends to have a slightly wider definition.
Distance travelled	Distance travelled refers to a measure of the progress made by an individual **beneficiary** while participating in a project. It is usually measured by highly specific questioning either through an interview or questionnaire. Sophisticated measures of distance travelled try to restrict the measurement to those factors most directly related to the goals of the individual concerned, and those measurable improvements that can be attributed at least in part to the work of the project rather than outside factors. Further information on measuring distance travelled and **soft outcomes** can be found on page 182.
Eligible expenditure	This refers to spend within the project that follows the financial guidelines for the particular funding scheme. A project team might also spend money that can't be reclaimed from the funding scheme – for example fees to consultants for writing further bids. In this case the organisation running the project would have to pay for this expense itself as the expenditure would be ineligible.
ESOL	English for Speakers of Other Languages. There are various standard qualifications in ESOL.

What it says	What it means
Exit strategy	Many projects, especially larger ones, are asked to produce an exit strategy. This describes how the project team will plan to continue all or some of the work after the end of the funding period. It tends to be more used in *capital projects*, where funders are keen to see that the building or equipment will continue to be used in the longer term.
FRESA	A Framework for Regional Employment and Skills Action (FRESA) has been produced by each of the English regions. It describes how regional partners will work together to ensure that people in the region are equipped with appropriate skills to contribute to the regional economy. The focus is on both skills development and employment, and the overall goal is a 'healthy labour market'.
ICT	Information and Communications Technology is seen as central to many funding programmes. The involvement of ICT in projects can range from ensuring that people are trained in ICT skills, to the use of ICT within projects to give greater value for money – for example through the use of e-learning or the use of ICT systems for more efficient communication or record keeping.
Match funding	A number of major funding programmes will not provide 100% of the funding needed to run the whole project. Instead they provide a percentage of the overall costs. The remainder of the costs must be met through match funding. This can be provided in cash, through other sources of funding, or 'in kind', by the donation of resources such as staff time from one or more of the organisations involved in the project. All of the funding for the project, including the match funding, should be *eligible expenditure*. Match funding in kind needs to be clearly accounted for.
National Qualifications Framework	The National Qualifications Framework (NQF) sets national standards for qualifications at all levels from entry level (the most basic qualifications) through to Level 8 (Doctoral level). The revised NQF was set in place on 1 September 2004. All nationally recognised qualifications in the UK should fit into this framework.

What it says	What it means
NEET	'Not in Education, Employment or Training' is a definition usually applied to the 16-19 age group. Young people in the NEET category are a particular target for support by a range of partners including Connexions and the Learning and Skills Councils.
Outputs	Clearly measurable achievements of a project can be referred to as outputs. Other terms that can be used include outcomes, deliverables or targets. 'Outputs' is usually used to describe the particular achievements that the funding body wish to see. These could include the number of people achieving qualifications, the number of people entering employment, the number of businesses assisted etc.
Returners to the labour market	People can take a break from the labour market and then return for a variety of reasons. Perhaps the most common is women returning after a break to have children, but increasingly both men and women take time out for other reasons, including care of other dependants.
Revenue project/funding	Revenue funding will only pay for the running costs of projects, such as staff, utilities and consumables, and will not contribute to investment in buildings or equipment (see **capital project/funding**). Projects that only need revenue funding are sometimes referred to as revenue projects.
Sectors	Some funding schemes are aimed at helping businesses, employees or potential employees in particular sectors – for example tourism, health and social care, or retail. The word sector can also be used to refer to the difference between, for example, the private, public, education, voluntary or community sectors. This can be important, as some funds are restricted as to which of these sectors can access them – for example some funds can only be used by the 'not-for-profit sector'.
Skill shortages	In some areas of the country, people with particular skills or qualifications are in short supply. For example, there has been a shortage of qualified nurses in many areas of the country. These are referred to as skill shortages. Funding is often targeted at training people to meet these skill shortages.

What it says	What it means
Social enterprise	A social enterprise is any kind of business venture that has a wider benefit to society than the creation of profit for individuals or shareholders. Examples include *community enterprise* where profit is ploughed back into the community, and businesses that result in genuine environmental benefits for the community.
Social exclusion	Social exclusion is difficult to define, but refers to the actual or potential exclusion of individuals or communities from the mainstream due to difficulties with housing, health, employment, educational achievement, family relationships etc. The results of social exclusion can include unemployment or low income, homelessness, poor mental health and a general vicious circle of deprivation for individuals and their families. Combating or preventing social exclusion is the goal of many funding organisations and schemes. More information about social exclusion can be found at: www.socialexclusion.gov.uk
Soft outcomes	In contrast to *outputs* the term 'soft outcomes' is used to describe the achievements of a project that are not easily countable but nonetheless are significant to the beneficiary group. These can include, for example, increased confidence or improved understanding of the labour market. Soft outcomes can be assessed and measured, and most funding schemes recognise them as being valid and significant. Further information on measuring soft outcomes and *distance travelled* can be found in page 182.
Sustainable development	The European Social Fund (ESF) requires that all projects address the need for sustainable development. Sustainable development has been defined by the EU as encompassing a combination of social, environmental and economic goals. This can include protection of the environment, opportunities for everyone and the provision of skills relevant to the current and future economy. All ESF projects are expected to address at least one of these areas, and preferably all three, in the way they are designed and delivered. Sustainable development is also becoming important for Lottery-funded projects. More information about sustainable development and the ESF can be found at www.esf.gov.uk/s_development/index.asp